EFFECTIVE TRAINING

a guide for the company instructor

D. R. Berry
Vice President & Director
Corporate Personnel Administration
Intext

ICS

International Correspondence Schools Division of Intext

Scranton, Pennsylvania 18515

First Printing .... February, 1968
Second Printing .... May, 1968
Revised Edition .... December, 1969

Author's Note

This book has been prepared to aid you in your role of an instructor in industry; to help you do a more effective job; and to help you achieve desired results. Upon completion of the study of this book, you should be able to perform the following tasks:

a. Given an assignment to arrange a training program, you will be able to arrange a meaningful, well-organized program.
b. Given a subject to present, you will be able to prepare a plan for presenting it.
c. Given a well-prepared lesson plan—or having developed one—you will be able to communicate the subject to others.
d. Given a subject to present, you will be able to select and develop effective communication aids for it.
e. Given a subject to present, you will be able to evaluate the effectiveness of your presentation and the response of the participants.
f. Given the assignment to conduct a session, you will be able to select and arrange a room for the most effective presentation.

a note about the author

Donald R. Berry is a graduate of the Wharton School, University of Pennsylvania, and received his B.S. Degree in Business Administration, magna cum laude, from the University of Scranton.

Mr. Berry is Vice President and Director of Corporate Personnel Administration for INTEXT. He has a vast experience in the fields of Systems and Procedures, Printing Production, New Product Planning, Marketing Research, and Stores and Traffic.

Mr. Berry is, in addition, a recognized authority in all phases of Training. He is in constant demand as speaker, guest lecturer, and—preeminently—Seminar Leader. The techniques and training rationales discussed in "Effective Training" have been used by Mr. Berry, with literally thousands of trainees, ranging from foremen to company presidents. The publishers are proud to pass these along, in permanent form, to all who share the author's interest in—and dedication to—the art of Training.

Contents

1

Planning the Training Program

Preliminary Planning

As an instructor, you may be asked to set up a complete training program, including preparation of the subject matter to be covered; deciding who will attend, where the sessions will be held, and how the subject will be presented; and many other details.

All of the details combine to make up the program. If they are all executed well, your program should run smoothly and be successful. Planning and preparation are musts; you cannot get along without them. Careful, thorough preparation will (1) help the participants derive maximum benefit from the sessions; (2) create a feeling that the program is important and worthwhile; and (3) give you more confidence, both in yourself and in the program.

As you think about the program, here are some questions to consider:

What are the objectives of the program?
Who should attend the program?

1

What?

When?

Why?

Where?

Who?

How?

THE PROGRAM

What is the background and experience of those who should attend?

What information do the participants need to receive prior to the program?

How will they receive the information?

Where will the program be conducted?

What facilities are available?

What arrangements must be made for facilities and equipment?

What housing or travel arrangements must be made for the participants?

How will the participants be informed about all arrangements?

Establishing Objectives

The objective or objectives of the program will determine what is to be done and how it is to be done. Objectives are the goals that you must attain. They are clear statements of purpose. You should determine objectives and keep them in mind throughout the planning and execution of the sessions.

Your objectives should be expressed in terms the participants understand, so that they will know exactly what they are expected to accomplish. These objectives should be written in terms of developing skills, knowledge, understanding, appreciation, and attitudes.

Objectives should be stated as specifically and definitely as possible, leaving no room for misinterpretation. The objectives should indicate the kind of behavior or performance which will be accepted as proof that the participant has achieved the objective. If you include in the objectives the conditions under which the behavior will be expected to occur and how well the participant must perform, your objective will be more specific and meaningful.

In writing objectives, use specific words such as *to write, to identify, to solve, to list, to compare.* These are preferable to vague phrases such as *to know, to understand, to appreciate,* which are not explicit or definite.

You will have general or overall objectives for the entire program, and immediate objectives for each session of the program. In the Author's Note to this book, you will find its objectives stated; these can be used as guides for your objectives. Notice that they are expressed in terms of *you*.

Your first step in planning a program, therefore, is to establish objectives—i.e., your destination. At the first session you should tell the group what the objectives are—let the participants know the destination. This will let them know what you are doing, help them relate the material to their own needs, and motivate them. Also, the participants will be able to evaluate their progress as the program continues.

Your objectives will also help you prepare a logical presentation. Once you know where you want to go, you can determine your starting point and the steps you need to take to get to your destination. What you're doing is making an analysis of what the participants must learn in order to reach the destination. It's like preparing for a trip. Once you know the destination, you can plan how to get there—what routes to take, how much time to allow, etc.

It's a good idea to write down what the participants need to learn or know in order to attain the objectives. As you do this, list any *related* information that is required. This will help you in arranging the individual sessions, so that you'll start at the beginning, based on what participants already know, and advance step by logical step.

Who Should Attend?

You may or may not have the responsibility for determining who will attend the session or sessions. Ideally, the group should be made up of individuals with approximately the same education, experience, background, and—insofar as possible—the same needs. This, of course, is seldom possible. But the participants should be actively concerned or involved with the subject; they should be individuals who will benefit from the program.

It will be helpful for you, the instructor, to know as much about your group as you can. Answers to questions such as the following will help you plan and present your material:

How many persons will attend?
What are their ages?
What is their education?
How much do they know about the subject to be presented?
How long have they been working for the company?
Are they attending voluntarily? (If they are required to attend, you will need to do more motivating.)

The more information you can get about the group, the more meaningful you can make your presentation to them.

Facilities

Select a location that provides as many of the following benefits as possible:

Look for a room that is adequate in size and well ventilated, to insure the comfort of your class. Remember that concentration promotes more smoking than usual: crowded classrooms must be ventilated. Find out whether or not doors and windows can be left open without the risk of outside noise becoming a distraction. Try to make arrangements to have these distractions eliminated during class. Noise level can be a crucial factor in the success of your program: even the best prepared instructor has difficulty competing with distracting noises.

Heating and air conditioning are frequent sources of problems, so you should check to make sure that you can control them. You and you alone should be in charge of regulating the temperature: if every individual has the right to change the thermostat to suit himself, you will have a problem. It's a good idea to arrange the tables and chairs so that no one will be sitting in a draft. If there is a draft, readjust the air vents or have them adjusted accordingly. Well before class time, make certain that the air conditioning is operating.

Avoid folding room dividers whenever possible. If sound proofing is a problem, investigate the possibility of scheduling your class during periods when adjoining rooms will not be in use. If several locations are available to you, make a few tests before making your selection.

Unless your classroom has been specifically designed for training classes, lighting will most likely be a problem. It is your responsibility to see to it that all communication aids are well lighted and can be easily seen. In addition, those in attendance must have adequate lighting to take notes, complete assignments, etc. Whenever projection equipment is being used, it must be possible to darken the room to an acceptable level. Unless the room is equipped with black-out shades, it's a good idea to check the light level before your meeting.

Seating and table arrangements are dependent upon the type of program you are conducting. Tables and chairs can be arranged in U or V shape. (Suggested seating and table arrangements are shown in Figs. 1, 2, and 3.) If you, as the leader, take a position opposite the door, latecomers will be less distracting. Don't spread your group out across the entire width of a room; this makes it difficult for you to see both sides of the group, and for the group to see your communication aids. If the group is large, it is better to arrange them according to the length of the room. Tables should be of sufficient width to provide adequate space for work books, name cards, and other appurtenances. Use the most comfortable chairs available. Vinyl-covered chairs, although extremely durable, become quite hot and uncomfortable with extended use and can become a distracting influence. (To help avoid discomfort, plan a ten-minute break during the session.)

Other provisions for the comfort and convenience of the members of the conference should be arranged. Make sure that there is an ash tray at each place, and arrange that they be emptied during the break. If the program runs over two hours, drinking water and glasses should be provided, and the pitchers should be replenished with fresh water during the break.

FIGURE 1. U Shaped Arrangement

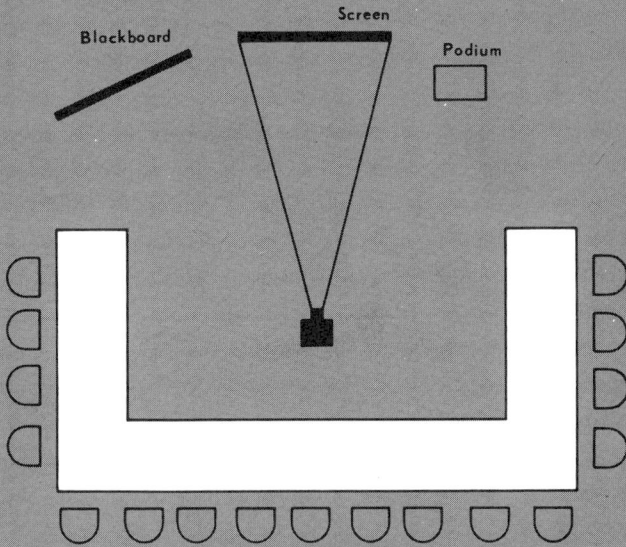

Blackboard   Screen   Podium

FIGURE 2. V Shaped Arrangement

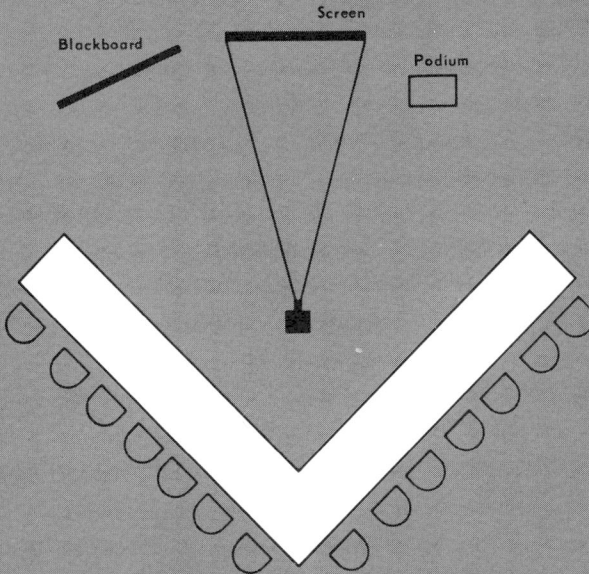

Blackboard   Screen   Podium

FIGURE 3. Other Arrangements

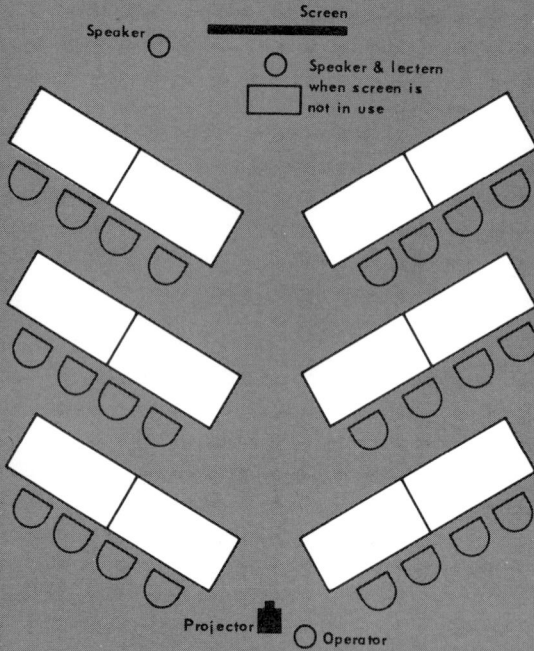

AUDITORIUM ARRANGEMENT
20 or more people
12 or more tables

NOTE: ALL DIAGRAMS DEPICT 72" ×30"
TABLES OF DESK HEIGHT

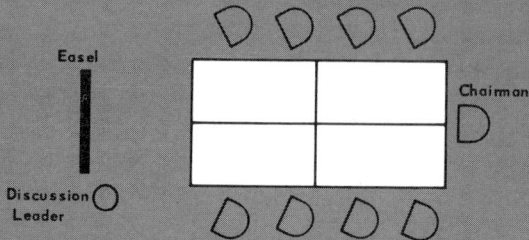

CONFERENCE TABLE ARRANGEMENT
12 or fewer people
4 or fewer tables

8

Carefully check the room size and acoustics to determine whether or not you will need a sound system. If your program includes group discussion, a two-way sound system may be necessary. If so, make *sure* you test it to avoid the possibility of feedback. Do this *before* the session.

You'll also want to be certain that there's a place for hats and coats, and that everyone knows the location of the room where the sessions will be held and the exact time when the sessions begin.

Adequate electric outlets should be at convenient locations to avoid the use of long extension cords. If these must be used, they should be securely taped to the floor with two-inch masking tape to reduce the possibility of anyone tripping over them.

Most instructors prefer to work from a podium. If you use a podium, it should be equipped with a small light to enable you to refer to notes when the room is darkened.

Through careful planning and preparation, your meeting room will establish the professional atmosphere that should be maintained throughout the entire program.

Materials

Carefully inspect and test in advance all projectors or recorders that you may require. If your program depends upon the use of a projector, be sure to have spare bulbs on hand. Also, it's a good idea to familiarize yourself with the method of changing these bulbs. There is nothing more embarrassing than to have a lamp failure and to have to start thumbing through an instruction book during a presentation. Have an extension cord handy; you may need it. Remember all tape recorders do not operate in the same way. Before you meet with your group, you should practice using all mechanical aids until you are able to use them efficiently.

Arrange the projection screen so that it is in position—ready to be used.

A pointer can be of great assistance during the presentation of slides or view-graphs.

Make sure that the blackboard is clean and that you have an adequate supply of chalk and an eraser.

If you want your students to take notes, provide them with pads and sharpened pencils, or request that they bring them. In the latter case, it is wise to have extras on hand.

Be certain that you have all materials assembled for distribution, and that you have enough copies for everyone.

It's a good idea to have a checklist of the items to be used and distributed. Review it before each session. A sample checklist is shown in Fig. 4.

Certificate of Achievement

You will probably want to give each participant a card or certificate indicating successful completion of the program. You should have these printed in advance. The names of the individuals can be typed in during the course of the program. The certificates or cards may be presented at the completion of the last session or at a special "awards" dinner or luncheon. A word of congratulations from a company official may be in order at this time, in addition, of course, to your own congratulations.

Tell the individuals at the beginning of the program that certificates will be awarded. If there are any requirements, such as attendance at a certain percentage of the sessions, let the individuals know what these terms are.

Publicity

You may also have to arrange for publicity in the local newspaper or the company house organ. If a photographer is available, a picture of the group can add to the interest value of a news article. The photograph will be of interest to members

Have you

1. Publicized the program or activity?

2. Informed everyone concerned about the time, place, location, and other meeting arrangements?

3. Arranged all details of the meeting room?

4. Checked the physical requirements for conducting the session?
   a. Seating arrangement
   b. Podium
   c. Ash trays
   d. Drinking water
   e. Coat racks
   f. Ventilation, heat, light, class comfort
   g. Projectors, screens
   h. Blackboard, chart pad, easel
   i. Chalk, crayon, eraser
   j. Papers, pencils

5. Secured the necessary aids and equipment?
   a. Charts
   b. Handouts
   c. Demonstration materials
   d. Record-keeping items
   e. Films
   f. Slides

6. Checked to be certain equipment is in working order, and familiarized yourself with it?

7. Established the objective for the session?

8. Carefully studied the lesson plan?
   a. Determined important points to be emphasized?
   b. Considered anticipated responses and group re-actions?
   c. Considered experiences, examples and stories to be used?

9. Developed enthusiasm for the program?

FIGURE 4. Check List For Instructor Preparation And Planning

of the group also; they may want to purchase copies, and you should arrange for them to be able to do so. The photograph can also become a part of your record of the program.

Records

You should keep attendance records for the program, checking attendance at the beginning of each session. You can check off the names or call the roll at the beginning of each session, or you can circulate an attendance sheet at the beginning of the session and let everyone present sign it; you can then check attendance later. If you use this method, be certain everyone signs the sheet.

If examinations are used, keep a record of grades.

Any comments you have on the participants or on the program itself should be part of your records also.

Keep a copy of all your plans, so that, with modification, you can use them for future sessions.

2

The Learning Process

What Is Learning?

If you look up the word "learning" in a dictionary, you will find one or more of the following definitions:

(a) knowledge acquired by systematic study in any field or fields of scholarly application;

(b) the act or process of acquiring knowledge or skill;

(c) the modification of behavior through interaction with the environment.

To comprehend fully the meaning of learning you should analyze the definitions. You'll notice that knowledge and skill are involved in learning; also, that learning is the act or process of acquiring. This indicates that learning is an active process; it cannot be passive. Learning, too, means acquiring knowledge or skill. Therefore, learning is more than being exposed to something. *Learning hasn't taken place until the knowledge and skill are developed and put to work*. Learning implies a

13

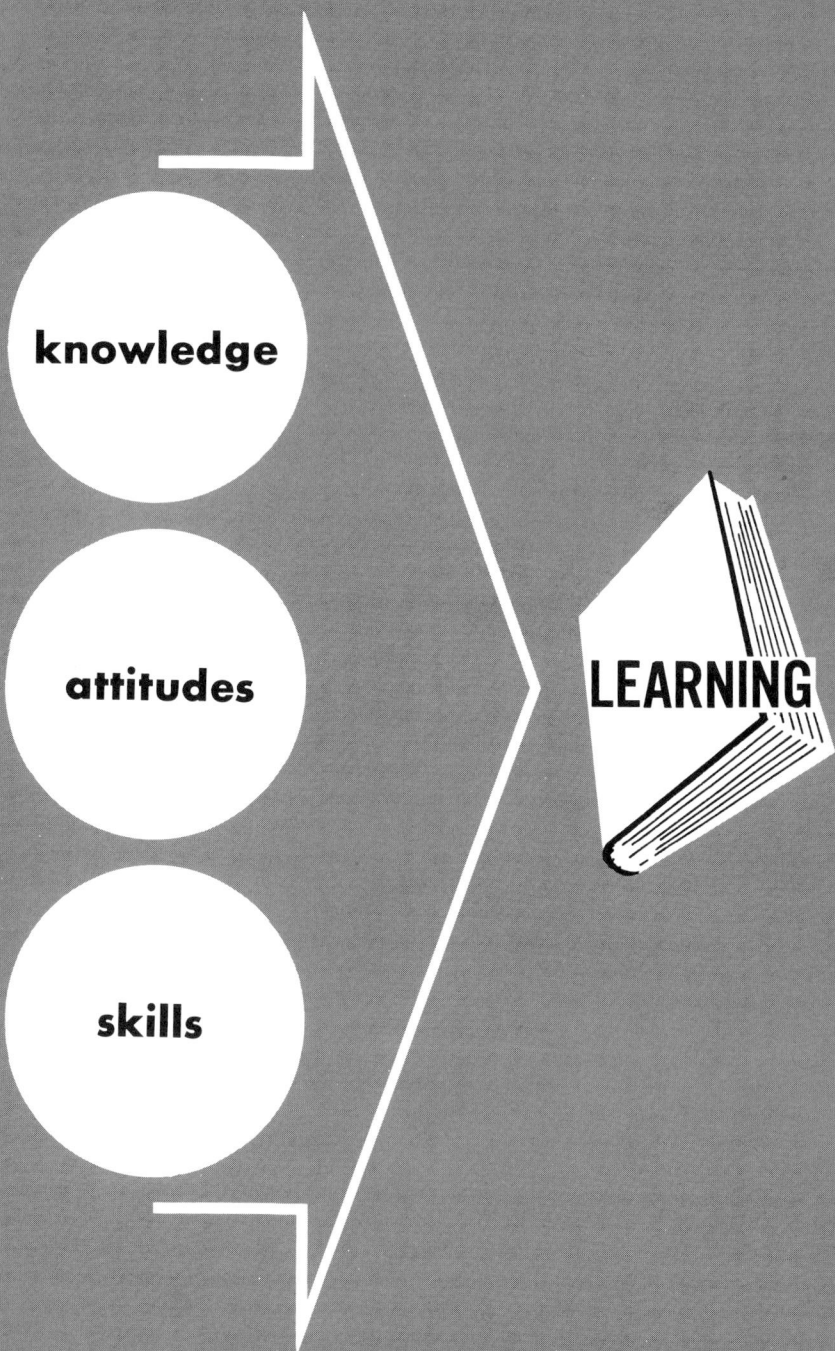

knowledge

attitudes

skills

LEARNING

change for the better—a modification of behavior, the acquisition of knowledge or skills. It is an active, positive process accomplished through the individual's own efforts.

A simple definition of learning—one that is easy to keep in mind—is: *Learning is the process of acquiring skills, knowledge, and/or attitudes.*

Types of Learning

As the definition implies, there are three types of learning. One kind of learning is acquiring knowledge or understanding —gaining ideas, principles, concepts, or facts.

Another type of learning involves the acquisition of abilities or skills. This may refer to either mental or physical abilities or skills, such as specific habits or ways of doing things.

A third type of learning is the acquisition of attitudes—of interests, appreciations, and ideals.

Of course, all three types of learning are related and may occur even though the training is directed at only one type of learning. For example, you may be interested in having an individual learn new abilities or skills: however, by improving an individual's skill (or way of *doing* something), a change in understanding and/or attitudes may also occur.

How Learning Is Achieved

Learning is accomplished through the five senses: seeing, hearing, feeling, smelling, and tasting. It is through these senses that impressions, which result in learning, are made on the mind. It is important, therefore, that you as an instructor present all material so that strong impressions are made on the trainee.

If you were to rank the senses in the order of importance in grasping impressions and ideas, the rating would be: seeing, hearing, feeling, smelling, and tasting. While the latter two are generally of least importance in giving impressions that are important for learning, they can be very important in some areas. For example, a fireman may use his sense of smell to learn the exact location of a fire; a food inspector in a plant may use his sense of taste to determine if a product is satisfactory and safe.

In planning any learning activity, it is important to remember that the five senses are the channels through which an individual is stimulated. Through the senses he makes contact with the things around him, and makes responses which lead to the acquiring of new knowledge, skills, or attitudes. Furthermore, the more senses involved, the greater the intensity of the learning.

How Adults Learn

The old theory that adults can't learn as easily as children has been disproved by modern research. Adults *can* learn effectively —and at all ages. However, the way in which adults learn differs significantly from the way in which children do. And to be an effective instructor, it is important that you know how adults learn.

Here are some points to keep in mind when you teach adults:

(a) Adults must *want* to learn. Children will learn something because someone—a teacher, a parent—says they should. Or, they will study simply to avoid getting a failing grade, even though the subject holds little interest for them. Adults, however, will not learn something just because someone says they should: they must have a desire to learn a new skill or to acquire knowledge.

(b) Adults will learn only when they feel a need to learn. They are practical in their approach to learning: they want to know how the training is going to help them— now. They are not interested in something that may be of value ten years from now. (Sometimes, through counseling, adults can be persuaded to learn something for their future good, but they'll learn more quickly when they expect immediate benefits.)

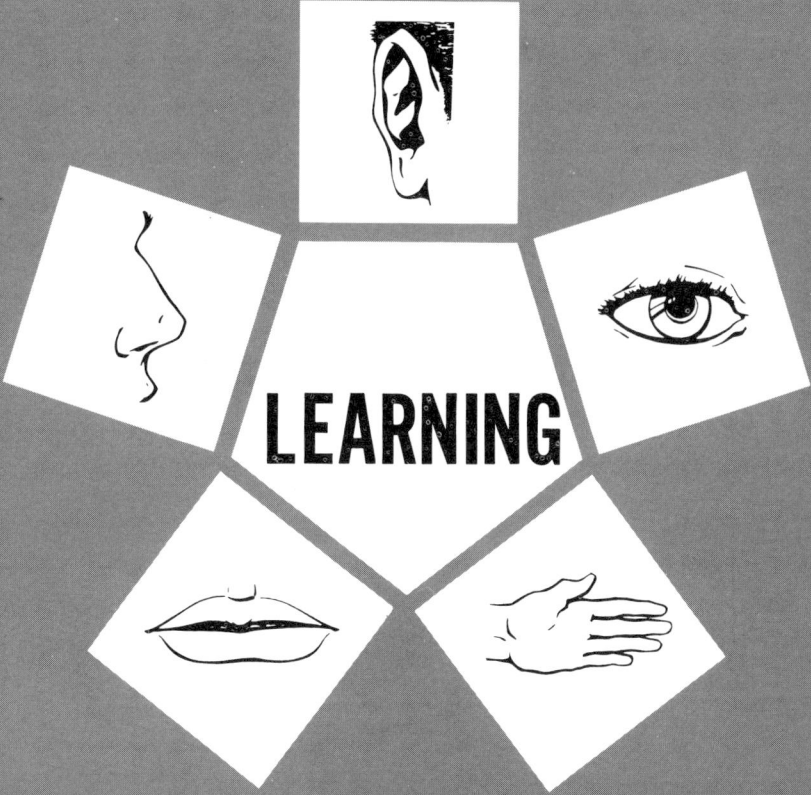

LEARNING

This means also that adults want to learn something from each training session. It's important that adults leave a learning situation with the feeling that they have gained something useful from it. In addition, adults quickly become impatient with too much theory or background: they respond best if you teach them, simply and directly, what they want to learn.

(c) Adults learn by doing. Research has shown that if adults immediately practice what they have learned, and continue to use it, learning retention is much higher. Studies have shown that if adults do not have opportunities to be involved actively in learning, within a year they will forget 50% of what they learned in a passive way—i.e., by reading or listening. In two years, they will have forgotten 80%. In fact, some studies indicate that *within 24 hours* they will have forgotten 50% of what they heard the previous day, and, within two weeks, an additional 25%.

Adults can learn by listening and watching, but they'll learn better—that is, more rapidly and with a higher level of retention—if they are actively involved in the learning process. This explains why adults should be encouraged to discuss a problem, think out a solution, practice a skill. Adults must have the opportunity to use what they learn, before they forget it or dismiss it from their memory.

(d) Adults learn by solving realistic problems. If the problems are not realistic—not true to life—adults will not work on them. Practical, realistic problems should be presented.

(e) Experience affects adult learning. Adults relate their learning to what they already know. If the new knowledge doesn't fit in with previous knowledge, they will probably reject or dismiss it.

Adults have had more experience than children, which can be an asset or a liability: an asset, when they have more opportunities to relate new learning to what is known; a liability, when the new knowledge does not relate to new learning.

Learning is based on experience. Therefore, when adults are confronted with a new experience, they interpret it on the basis of past experience. Thus, any new information or skills must be related to what the individuals already know. In other words, adults build learning on what is known.

(f) Adults learn best in an informal environment. If the environment is too much like a classroom, adults will not learn as well. Many adults have unpleasant memories of their school days; others feel they have finished school, and they do not care to be reminded of it. Also, if the environment is too "school-like," adults are likely to think the whole situation is childish. Consequently, the meeting place should be set up as informally as possible. Arranging the chairs in a V or U and permitting smoking (if there are no regulations against it) help to remove the inhibiting classroom atmosphere.

(g) Adults respond to a variety of teaching methods. Like children, they learn better if an idea is presented in many ways—in other words, when the information reaches them through more than one sensory channel. Of course, the method used will depend on what is being taught and on the desired objectives.

(h) Adults want guidance, not grades. True, adults want to know how they are doing—what progress they are making. This is important to them, but grades or tests may be frightening. Adults tend to shy away from tests because of the fear of being humiliated, of not doing well. They may believe that they will not do well because they have been out of school too long, or that they are "too old to learn." Still, they want reassurance that they are making satisfactory progress—that they are on the right track. Adults can and will measure their own progress. However, many times the standards they set for themselves are too high, and they become discouraged. Sincere praise and guidance from the instructor will help prevent this.

The Instructor's Role

As you have read before, learning is an active, positive process accomplished through the individual's own activity. You, as the instructor, contribute to the learning process by acting as the agent who makes things happen. The change may be in things known (knowledge); it may be in comprehension (understanding); it may be in things valued (appreciation); it may be in things done (skills); it may be in things wanted (interest). Your function is to promote change in those whom you are instructing. If this is not done, you have not accomplished your purpose—there has been no learning.

Remember that you actually teach people, not a subject. The subject matter of the class is really the student, not the knowledge. Your knowledge is your tool, the means by which you make things happen; your knowledge is not the product. If the tool is skillfully used, then the participant's needs will be met, and you will have taught.

3

Communication

Definition

Communication is the imparting or conveying of knowledge or information. It is a mutual exchange of facts, thoughts, opinions and/or emotions involving presentation and reception. In other words, there must be presentation and there must be reception of what is presented if the communication is to be complete. The "circuit" must be completed. Without the two elements—presentation and reception—you do not have communication.

Importance of Communication to an Instructor

The ability to communicate effectively is very important to you as an instructor, because it is through communication that you make things known to your students. You have heard the comment, "He knows his subject, but he can't get it across." The inability to "get it across" is due to the instructor's failure to communicate. Unless you can express your ideas clearly and fluently; can make yourself understood; and can develop and maintain interest, you will not be an effective instructor.

As an instructor you want to get things done—you want to make things happen. This is your role as an agent of change. Communication is the means by which you accomplish this. Without effective communication there will be no instruction; there will be no teaching.

Methods of Communication

Two methods of communication—oral and written—are usually thought of in any consideration of the subject.

Oral communication means, of course, communication through the spoken word. It is the method you use in conversation—in your work and in your social life. It is the most direct method of communication, particularly on a face-to-face basis. You will make extensive use of oral communication in conducting sessions and meetings.

Written communication refers to that which is in writing—letters, memoranda, telegrams. You may use written notes, problems, case studies, and handouts as supplements to your oral communication. However, in conducting training sessions written communication will not be your primary method of communication.

In addition to these two methods, an instructor can communicate by using visual and audio devices. These take many forms, such as charts, signs, flashing lights, bells, pictures—even gestures, facial expressions, one's manner of walking or sitting. Some of these supplement or aid in the communication; others are *methods* of communication. Some represent a conscious effort to communicate; others do not. Much depends on how each device is used. For example, a picture may be used to supplement what has been said—or it may be used to communicate the complete idea, without any explanation. Some of the techniques mentioned, such as gestures or facial expressions, can be used in conjunction with oral communication; many of these may be unconscious. Thus, unless you are careful, you may accidentally communicate the wrong idea. Your frown or scowl may be interpreted as dissatisfaction with the group, or with an individual, or with a particular comment. A gesture may be distracting, rather than helpful, by taking attention away from what is being said.

It is important for you to remember that communication involves more than just speaking or writing. You communicate with all parts of yourself—the way you talk, your posture, your facial expressions, your tone of voice—as well as by *what* you say. Communication is a continuous process, not something you start and stop, or turn on or off. You communicate even when you are silent—sometimes very tellingly.

If you keep this in mind, you will communicate more effectively. You will concentrate on doing that which aids you in communciation, and avoid that which detracts or antagonizes. Also, you will be more perceptive of the group—will be able to understand them better—and will be able to help them communicate more fully with you.

How to Communicate Effectively

As noted above, everything that you do affects your communication: it is not possible to separate communication from the entire process of instruction. No matter what aspect of the instruction process is being considered, communication is involved.

However, there are certain communication guidelines that should be mentioned:

(a) Use clear, simple language. Words are the symbols by which you convey your ideas. To be understood, therefore, you should use words which best express the meaning you have in mind. In selecting your words, strive to use those that have the same meaning for you as for the listener. These are usually specific words—words that may be termed "labels."

For example, you and your listener share the same understanding of the words *empty, inch, impossible.*

23

COMMUNICATION

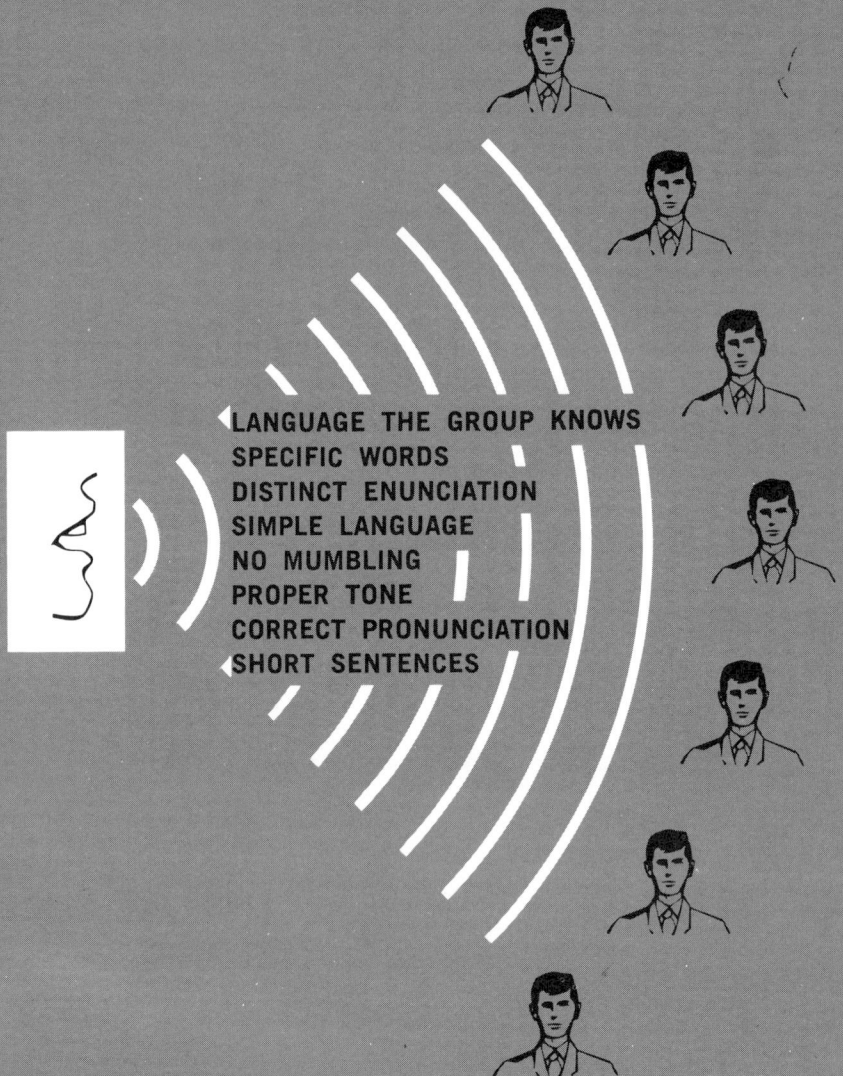

LANGUAGE THE GROUP KNOWS
SPECIFIC WORDS
DISTINCT ENUNCIATION
SIMPLE LANGUAGE
NO MUMBLING
PROPER TONE
CORRECT PRONUNCIATION
SHORT SENTENCES

Words such as *big, hard, cold, easy,* and *difficult* require interpretation on the part of the listener: what may be *big* to one person may be *small* to another. The listener is forced to place his own meaning on the word.

(b) Use language the group understands. To communicate effectively, you should adapt your language to the academic and intellectual level—and to the age level—of the group. You should "talk their language." This accomplishes two things: It insures that the group will understand you, and it establishes rapport. If there is terminology peculiar to the particular subject or group, it should be used—though this does not mean slang or off-color language. It *does* mean correct English that can be understood by the group. Also, technical terms which may be new to the group should be explained.

It is better to over-simplify, as far as words are concerned, than to risk misunderstanding. In other words, talk to *ex*press, not *im*press. If participants do not understand you, they will lose interest quickly. If they misunderstand, they may become confused.

(c) Use specific words. When specific words are used, there is little opportunity for misunderstanding or misinterpretation. For example, if you say, "Tuesday at 1 P.M.," you are being specific. If you say "a while back," there's room for private interpretation on the part of the listener. "A while back" may be interpreted as an hour ago, six hours ago, a day before, a week ago—even ten years ago! If you attempt to explain by saying, "Something like this," you are not being specific. Each listener will put his own interpretation on it. Or if you say "and so forth," you are not being specific—each listener will determine for himself what is meant.

You should keep in mind that your words may not evoke the same image in someone else's mind that they do in yours: use words that are as specific in meaning as possible.

(d) Use short sentences. Short sentences which are logical and clear are more easily understood. A long sentence may be too wordy, too difficult to follow. The listener gets tired or forgets what was said in the beginning. Your sentences should be constructed of specific, direct words that are put together in a clear, accurate, logical manner.

Be certain to indicate the end of your sentences by dropping your voice.

(e) Speak to be understood. It is essential that you be heard to be understood. Your enunciation should be distinct; your pronunciation correct. There should be no mumbling, no "er" or "ah"-ing. Your rate of speaking should be appropriate to the material; neither too fast nor too slow. Your tone of voice should be friendly and sincere. You should be conversationally direct, remembering that you are really talking with the group, not to them. Don't let your voice portray an indifferent, impersonal attitude.

As an instructor you will be effective if you remember that you communicate in everything that you do and that words have one purpose—to transmit intelligence. Also, remember that words in themselves mean nothing: it is people who give meaning to them.

4

Planning the Individual Session

The Reasons for Planning

Planning and organization are essential if a program is to be a success. Very often the unsuccessful leader is the unorganized leader. Careful planning insures a logical approach and an orderly and effective presentation.

Planning involves thinking out acts and purposes beforehand, enabling you to give a logical, coherent presentation. Your group will know what is going on and where the presentation is going, and will be able to follow and understand it. If there is no organization—if material is presented in a random fashion —the group will have difficulty figuring out the meaning. It is a leader's responsibility to present material in such a way that the group can understand it: just having facts isn't enough. They must be presented and put together in such a way that the meaning is clear. From beginning to end, the presentation must be held together in a smoothly connected series of ideas, facts, opinions, details, and generalizations.

Remember, the subject is familiar to you; it is apt to be new to your group. They need facts, plus a scheme of organization which will help them to understand the material.

To plan, you must know your objective or purpose: Why is the session being conducted? What do you want the participants to learn? What aspects of the subject are to be presented now? What does the group need to know? What is the best way to present the material? Answers to these questions are all part of planning.

A plan for each session will keep you on the right track, pointed toward your goal. You'll be less likely to stray from the subject. In addition, you'll retain time control: you'll know how much time to devote to each phase. You won't spend too much time on one aspect and not enough on another.

Your plan will also give you confidence. You will *know* you are ready to do a good job. (Also, you can have the plan in note form to refer to, if necessary.)

A review of the plan prior to each session will refresh your memory. The plan can also be filed, so that—if you present the material again—you won't have to prepare it a second time.

Types of Plans

There are many formats for session plans, but there are three basic ones. First, there is the topic outline (Fig. 5). This is the most common type of formal outline. In it, the main points and sub-topics are stated in brief phrases or single words.

The sentence outline is similar to the topic outline. The difference between the two is that in the sentence outline main and subordinate points are expressed in complete sentences rather than in brief phrases or words.

The third type is known as an instructor's manuscript. More detailed than the outline, it includes everything that is to be done and said during a session. The preparation of an instruc-

Office Forms and Forms Control

I. Forms and business
    A. Important role of printed forms in modern business
    B. The need for scientific forms design
    C. Nature and classes of business forms

II. Factors to be considered in forms construction
    A. Methods of filling in and copying a form
    B. Types of paper used
    C. Different ways in which forms may be presented to users
    D. Tools needed to do form design work

III. Designing the form
    A. Five requirements of good form design
    B. Designing forms to meet these requirements
    C. Giving complete and specific instructions to the printer

IV. Forms Control
    A. Need for forms control program
    B. Method of organizing a forms control program
        1. Essential factors
        2. Basic steps in setting up program
    C. Relationship of forms control to management

FIGURE 5.

tor's manuscript takes more work and time than the preparation of an outline; however, it does insure thorough preparation and thorough analysis of the material. It also is better suited for review and for refreshing the instructor's memory. The instructor's manuscript is also beneficial if someone else is going to take over a session.

The first two—the topic and sentence outlines—require you to have a reasonably complete knowledge of the subject at the tip of your tongue; the user must also be able to work from notes.

How to Prepare Your Plan

The first step in making a plan is to select a title. This should be a brief but descriptive statement of the subject.

Second, the objectives of the session should be stated. These should be as complete and as specific as those for the entire program. What do you want the participants to learn during the particular session? What should they be able to do, and how proficient should they be in doing it, at the close of this session?

Third, you should include a detailed list of all equipment you'll need for the session. Don't rely on memory: it's easy to forget an obvious piece of equipment. A chalkboard is of no use without chalk. Yet, there have been instances where a chalkboard was requested and provided; however, because chalk was not requested, it was not supplied. So list everything, leaving nothing to "common sense."

You are now ready to plan your introduction—plan how you're going to start the session. It is in this section that you plan your motivation of the participants. Of course, you'll want to tell the group the topic for the session, and how you are going to present it. In doing this, you will tell the participants how they are concerned—how they will benefit. You'll relate the topic to them personally. This will help you get their interest—help you motivate them.

In your introduction give a preview of the session. This will not detract from the session. On the contrary, it will add to it, because you will be giving the group guidelines by means of which they can follow the material as it is presented. This will make it more meaningful for them.

Next, you will want to outline the subject as you are going to present it. You will arrange your presentation so that it is logical, starting with what is known and building on that. Remember, your group must be able to relate what is being presented to what they already know. It must fit in. If it does not, the group will be inclined to reject it.

In this portion— the body of your outline—you should include references to any communication aids that are to be used. This will insure your using them at the proper time.

You can also include questions that you plan to ask, and expected responses. In other words, you will include what you are going to do; the expected activity of the participants; and the points you want to bring out.

A time control can also be incorporated into your plan. You should allot a specified amount of time to each main point; for example, you may allot five minutes to your introduction. In using the plan, you may find that you need only four minutes, so you use only four. You should be flexible in your time control; however, you should not have to make major adjustments if you have been realistic in preparing your time allotment.

Include in the body of your outline examples, illustrations, and personal experiences that will make your presentation more meaningful and interesting. These will also help to establish you as an authority in the field.

The last item in the plan is your summary. In it you will review the highlights and main points of the presentation. You should again point out how this material relates to the group.

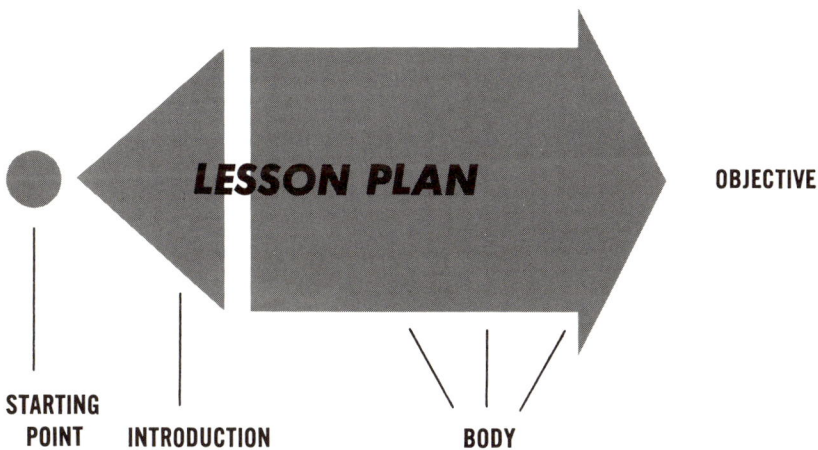

LESSON PLAN   OBJECTIVE

STARTING
POINT   INTRODUCTION   BODY

In your summary, tell the group what you are going to cover in the next session and remind them of the time and place. If there is any assignment for them, you should give it at this time.

If you want to suggest any supplementary reading on the subject you have covered, you can do this now. Quite often there are individuals in the group who will want to read additional material on the subject and who will appreciate this information.

A page of an instructor's manuscript is shown in Fig. 6.

Notes	Outline
	Before we start discussing what we can do to communicate more effectively, let's define communication.
Ask the class.	What does the word communication mean to you?
	1. Communication is the art of imparting or conveying knowledge or information. 2. Communication is the mutual exchange of facts, thoughts, opinions or emotions. 3. Communication involves presentation and reception.
Summarize discussion. Use Communication Aid #1.	If we give some thought to communication, we realize that communication is the means by which we accomplish results through other people. It can be defined as the art of imparting or conveying knowledge or information, such as facts, thoughts, opinions or emotions involving both presentation and reception.

FIGURE 6.

Using The Plan

In developing the plan for the session, you made a thorough analysis of the subject. You acquired a good background of information and undoubtedly did considerable reading of reference material. Also, you considered the best way to present the material, including the development of a logical approach. All of this preparation should give you confidence in your ability to conduct the session.

Keeping the plan in front of you will also give you confidence. However, it should not be used as a crutch. Don't read the plan word for word; use it merely as a guide, which you adapt to the group's needs.

The plan is not a substitute for thinking. During the sessions you will also need to analyze the contributions from the participants, as well as evaluate the session as you progress. You may discover that you need to change to a different technique or method. You can do this painlessly if you are thoroughly prepared.

5

Communication Aids

What Are Communication Aids?

Communication aids may be visual devices or audio-visual devices. Visual aids are anything which involve communication media which utilize sight. They range from the very simple to the complex.

Audio-visual aids, which combine hearing and sight, are becoming more and more popular.

Why Use Communication Aids?

Perhaps few things are more difficult than trying to convey an idea from one individual to another. Usually, you will use words to do so. No matter how carefully you select and arrange the words, however, there can be different interpretations. A visual aid can help to prevent misunderstandings.

Visual media are helpful in reinforcing or in illustrating the spoken word. This is because these aids appeal to more than one sense. The combination of hearing and seeing is a more effective learning formula than is hearing alone. A stimulus is more lasting when it is presented to hearing and sight at the same time. Therefore, when you talk *and* show, via a visual aid, your chances of being understood are doubled. You also double the possibility of being remembered.

Visual aids also provide a change of pace, which helps to maintain interest and attention by keeping the presentation from becoming monotonous.

Visual aids also save time. You've heard the expression, "A picture is worth ten thousand words." Many times it is just that valuable. A visual aid can often present material much more clearly, thoroughly, and quickly than any number of words. A visual aid can portray, more effectively, in a few minutes what might take an hour or more of discussion. In fact, a whole day of talking may not say as much as one visual aid.

Add realism to your presentation by the use of visual aids. The participants can see what you are talking about. It is the next best thing to "being there."

Emphasis is provided when you use visual aids because you reinforce what you say. You are calling attention to main points, thus aiding in learning retention.

Also, by looking at something the participants become involved. This is a limited form of participation, but it does aid in understanding and retention.

The main benefit of communication aids is that they permit you to appeal to more than one sense at a time. This results in clearer understanding and greater retention.

When to Use Communication Aids

You use visual aids to underscore a main point or points, and to reinforce instruction.

You, as an instructor, must decide if a visual aid will add to your presentation. A visual aid should not be used for its own sake; it must serve a purpose. And it must be relevant to the material you are presenting; if it is irrelevant, it will divert your audience's attention.

Types of Communication Aids

An instructor has a vast array of visual aids from which to choose. In selecting one, you should choose that which most effectively does the job you want it to do. There are advantages and disadvantages to all aids.

Let's consider the most commonly used visual aids.

a) *Chalkboard or blackboard*

The blackboard or chalkboard is probably the best known visual aid. It is a simple aid, especially when compared to some of the fancy devices on the market.

The blackboard is inexpensive and quite versatile. Because it permits spontaneity in presentation, it is often used to develop a topic with the group; to list problems; and to record progress. It can be used for anything in which you want the participants to take part. Since erasing is simple, changes can be made very easily. Usually blackboards or chalkboards provide a large writing area.

A disadvantage of the blackboard is that if you want any of the material saved, you must copy it. Also the material usually cannot be prepared in advance.

If a blackboard is to be used, you should, if possible, plan what you are going to write. Even though you are going to develop a problem or topic with the audience, you should do some planning for the use of the blackboard. You should have a fairly good idea of the response you are going to get, so you can do some preliminary planning. In planning, try to do it so you will do a minimum of writing. Limit your writing to key words; it is not necessary to use complete sentences.

Neatness and clarity are important. Be certain your writing is legible and vivid enough so that everyone can see. You will find that printing is more legible than writing when you use chalk. Practice writing on the chalkboard so you can write or print in straight lines without the chalk squeaking.

On a blackboard you will probably use white chalk; on a green chalkboard, yellow. Other colors may be used, but they do have a disadvantage: they are not easily erased without washing the board.

You should not attempt to write on the blackboard and talk at the same time. If you do, you will find yourself talking to the blackboard rather than to your group. Also, when you face the blackboard you are not in a position to observe the reaction of your group. It is best to do your writing as quickly as possible, and then return your full attention to the group.

Try not to block anyone's view as you write. If, as you face your audience, you stand to the right of the board with your body at a 45° angle, you will be in a good position for writing. (See Fig. 7.) Stretch your right arm across your body so you can write easily. (If you are left-handed, work from the left side of the board.) When you have finished writing, place the chalk on the tray. It becomes a distraction if you keep it in your hands to play with.

If you are going to refer to the work that is on the board, use a pointer—your arm will block the view. Also, be certain you do not block the view of the board with your body. If you stand to the left of the board, you can use the pointer in your right hand and still face the entire audience. If you are left-handed, then stand to the right of the board. This will not only insure that you do not block anyone's view, but also will enable the members of the group to hear your voice without distortion. When you are through using the pointer, put it down; or, if you're going to use it within the next minute or two, hold it easily at your side.

FIGURE 7. Chalkboard

When the material on the board has served its purpose, remove it. It is no longer useful; on the contrary, it can be a distraction. Be certain you allow enough time for the members of the group to copy any blackboard material they wish—then erase it. Do not wait until you are ready to use the board again.

b) *Chart pad*

The chart pad usually consists of an easel to which a large* pad of paper can be attached (Fig. 8). A felt-tipped marker or grease pencil is best for writing on the chart pad, although regular crayon can be used.

The chart pad is used in much the same manner as the blackboard. However, erasing is not necessary; used pages are simply turned over. (This makes it possible to turn back the pages for review.)

---

* Usually 34″ x 28″.

FIGURE 8. Chartpad

Pages of the chart pad can be prepared in advance, which is often a definite advantage. If you want to prepare the pages in advance, but want to be certain that succeeding pages are not revealed until you are ready for them, leave every other page blank during your preparation. Another method to insure that points are not "telegraphed" until the right time is to use the paper strip takedown method. In this technique, the material is prepared in advance and each point covered by a paper strip. Two short strips of Scotch Tape or masking tape may be used to hold the strip loosely in place (Fig. 9). When you are ready to discuss each point, you remove the appropriate strip. This insures that the participants do not get ahead of you.

Pages from a chart pad can be torn off and clipped to holders around the room if desired. They may also be saved for future reference.

FIGURE 9.   Paper Strip Take Down Method

The limitations of a chart pad, as compared to a blackboard, are its smaller size and the impossibility of erasure: you must either turn to a new page and start over, which is time-consuming, or cross out and continue on the same page. Such scribbling out usually proves to be messy and distracting, and may also suggest inefficiency to the group.

Mechanically speaking, use the chart pad as you do the chalkboard. Don't talk to it; don't block the audience's view; don't write too much; don't play with the crayon or pointer. Write legibly and quickly, remembering to remove each page (or to turn it over) when you have finished with it.

Easels and pads are usually light-weight and portable. Some fold down into a small size for greater portability.

FIGURE 10. Chart

c) *Charts*

A chart is any poster or pre-prepared graphic device. It can be made of almost anything—photographs, diagrams, drawings, graphs, word messages, or a combination of these (Fig. 10). Charts are permanent and portable, and can be simple or very elaborate. However, you should remember that the idea portrayed is the important factor—not the artistry of the chart-maker.

Charts may be used alone, or in a series to tell a story. The paper strip take-down method can be used. Usually, however, only one idea is presented on a chart.

The same do's and don'ts apply to the use of charts as to chalkboards and chart pads.

FIGURE 11. Flannel Board

d) *Flannel board*

The flannel board—or flannel graph, as it is sometimes called—is simply a piece of flannel stretched over a board or a metal or wooden frame (Fig. 11). Words or sentence strips or pictures backed with flannel or fuzzy flock will hold on a flannel board that is inclined slightly from the vertical position. Relatively light items backed with masking tape or rough-grade sandpaper will also adhere to the flannel background. The fact that Styrofoam will also stick to flannel makes it possible to use three-dimensional items made from that product.

Flannel boards, which come in a variety of sizes, can be portable or permanent. Their main advantage is that they permit a step-by-step presentation. Items can be shifted or changed easily, thus enabling action or the shift-ing relationship between ideas to be shown. A diagram can be developed on flannel boards as you talk.

The items to be used, often called cutouts or slap-ons, may be prepared in advance; or they may be blank and covered with acetate, thus allowing you to write on them and erase the writing later.

In using the flannel board, you should organize your cutouts and rehearse with them before hand. In placing the cutout on the board, exert a slight pressure so that the cutout will stick. If the group is unfamiliar with the use of the flannel board, it may be advisable to explain how it works: the participants could be distracted from your presentation by their curiosity. You should, of course, face the group as you use the flannel board, taking care that you do not block anyone's view.

Flannel boards can be purchased, or you can easily construct your own. Flannel is available in any dry-goods or fabric store, and the frame is easily made. A portable flannel board can be made by fastening a piece of flannel to an ordinary window-shade roller. This can then be draped over an easel.

A flannel-less flannel board, so to speak, is even pos-sible, using velour cover stock for both board and cutouts. This makes a lightweight, portable device that serves quite well.

Magnetic boards are also available. These are like flannel boards, except that a metallic surface is used; the cutouts have little magnets taped to their backs.

e) *Overhead transparency projector*

The overhead projector permits the projection of items from transparencies. The transparencies may be pur-chased reprints made on special transparent paper, or

FIGURE 12.   Overhead Transparency Projector

they may be made by writing or drawing with grease pencil or special felt markers on acetate. Glass slides may
also be projected.

You may hear this type of projector referred to as an
"over-the-shoulder" projector (Fig. 12). This is because
the projector is placed in front of the audience, and the
image reflected on a screen above and behind the instructor. The projector is placed next to you, from 5 to 12'
from the screen. This permits you to operate the projector while facing the audience. Even if you want to
point something out, you do not need to turn around: you
can point to the item or items on the transparency itself.
You may also write on the slide, using color if you desire.
Markers are available which permit you to write on a

transparency and remove the writing when you have finished.

Transparencies are relatively easy to prepare. Their visibility and clarity are usually good. Also, overlays can be used, thus permitting a cumulative presentation.

Portable projectors and table-top models are available. Some fold into carrying cases for easier portability.

Although these projectors are equipped with a fan for cooling purposes, watch your transparency for signs of too much heat, evidenced by curling or browning of the transparency. Some transparencies are most sensitive to heat, particularly those with a great deal of ink, such as illustrations.

When you've finished with a transparency, always turn the projector off. In addition to reducing heat, you remove the image or the light, which might be a distraction. As you remove the transparencies, turn them over and file them one on top of the other, so that at the end of the presentation, your transparencies are in the proper order for re-use.

f) *Opaque projector*

The opaque projector (Fig. 13) is similar to an overhead projector. However, it is used to project opaque objects, such as book pages, photographs, drawings, letters, and small three-dimensional objects. It operates through the use of a series of mirrors, and no special preparation of materials is necessary. Usually any device up to 10″ x 10″ can be projected, if it is no more than an inch or two thick.

Also, you can use a roll of paper on which prepared messages can be written and cranked through the projector. This projector, too, should be turned off when not in use. Materials should not be exposed to projector heat for too long a period.

FIGURE 13. Opaque Projector

If you're going to project photographs, you should first adhere them to a piece of annealed glass that will not crack from heat. This will also keep the photographs flat. If you're projecting just one book page or a single sheet of paper, it's a good idea to mount it on a stiff piece of paper. This will insure its remaining flat and prevent curling. If the paper curls, it may be difficult to focus the sheet.

Three disadvantages of the opaque projector are (1) the room must be completely dark when you use the device; (2) the image projected is not very bright and it may be difficult for members of the group to see details; and (3) opaque projectors are usually quite bulky.

g) *Slide and filmstrip projector*

Slide and filmstrip projectors project transparent pictures onto a screen. Slides are individual pictures; filmstrips, series of pictures. Both are effective communication aids capable of projecting large, life-like images. Charts, diagrams, and pictures can be made into slides, or you can take and use actual on-the-screen photographs. These add realism to your presentation.

The slides are small, so storage space is not a problem. The projectors, too, are portable. Some are equipped with a remote-control device which permits you to change slides as you talk. The remote control panel may also provide for focusing. Some projectors focus each slide automatically.

A slide presentation requires a great deal of preparation and rehearsal. The slides should be carefully selected so that they convey your message accurately and adequately. You must be certain they are arranged in proper sequence. If you're going to have someone else run the projector, you must rehearse with him. Work out a cue system and practice. There are several ways you can do this: (1) You may say, when you've finished with one slide, "On the next slide . . . ". The operator listens for those words and moves the next slide into position. (2) You may use a wire connected to the operator's table: when you press a button, a light flashes in front of the operator, alerting him to project the next slide. (3) You may use a sound cue, a bell, a snapper, or simply the tapping of the pointer —although this crude type of cue system often emphasizes the partitioning of your presentation and does not permit as smooth a delivery.

The room should be at least partially darkened, so you must also arrange in advance for the lights to be turned off and on. Also, you may need a light on the lectern so you can see your notes. If so, be certain this light does not glare in your eyes or reflect on the screen.

If possible, arrange to stand on a raised platform beside the screen, using a pointer if you refer to the image on the screen. Do not point with your finger, as your body will cast a distracting shadow.

Your commentary must be developed to coincide with your slides. During your introductory remarks, leave the lights on and the projector off: otherwise, you will have a glaring light on the screen, which is distracting, and your projector may get too warm. Another disadvantage is that the people can't see you and you can't see them: this prevents you from studying the group—from building up an early rapport with them.

When you use slides, be certain to leave your pictures exposed long enough for your group to study them. Remember, each slide is new to your group: give them time to absorb it. (A rule-of-thumb is 3 to 5 slides per minute.) Also, make certain your commentary applies only to the picture on the screen. Once a picture is off the screen, forget it; don't bring it up again. Premature removal of slides indicates the need for further planning and better timing.

Avoid using too many slides. A too rapid succession of slides can be ineffective.

It is possible to combine slides with a tape-recorded narration. However, "live" (personal) narration is better. In any case, remember that attention wanders from a taped presentation more than five or six minutes long.

Slides and filmstrips are available from commercial sources. Filmstrips are difficult to produce on your own. If you use them, be certain you are familiar with them.

h) *Motion-picture projector*

A movie projector projects motion-picture films, with or without a sound track. Since it shows motion, it can be quite effective, presenting in a few minutes material which would take much longer to describe effectively in words. However, film is only effective if it is properly used.

First of all, you must be careful in selecting the film. You should be certain that it portrays what you want. This means previewing it carefully prior to use.

The film should be introduced—that is, you should "set the stage" for the presentation. Give the group an idea of what is coming—let them know what to watch for. This will not detract from the film: on the contrary, it will add to its effectiveness by providing guidelines.

Before the group convenes, make sure that all equipment is in working order. The projector should be threaded with the film. The screen should be in place, and focus adjusted. It is a good idea for you or your operator to know how to splice a film, in the event it breaks during the presentation.

If a sound track is used with the film, it is imperative that sound and picture be perfectly synchronized. Nothing is more ludicrous than sounds that do not match the action of the screen. It is important, also, to adjust the amplifiers to the conditions of your room. If the sound is too low, some members of your group will not hear the presentation; if too loud, you will lose precious time adjusting the amplifier while the film goes on.

After the film is over, you should conduct a discussion of it. Keep your objectives in mind; know the points you want to stress. You may start by asking prepared questions. This discussion will give the group a better understanding of the film, and provide them with an opportunity to relate it to their particular needs and desires. Or, you may wish to stop the film for discussion at some midway point or points. Some films are especially adapted to this technique, which helps to maintain interest and increase understanding. Attention is likely to wander from a film after ten to fifteen minutes of uninterrupted viewing.

Front- or rear-view projection may be used for slide, filmstrip, or movie presentation. For front-screen projection, you set up the projector in front of the screen, and shine the image on it. The room must be darkened, and you must avoid casting a shadow on the screen by standing or walking between screen and projector.

When you use rear-screen projection, you present slides, filmstrips, or films from *behind* the screen. Here, the image shines through the screen. This method requires a special screen, which may also be used for front-screen projection.

The advantages of rear-screen projection are:

1. The projector is eliminated from the audience's view. You don't have to worry about the hazards of wires in the room, or be concerned with anyone walking in front of the projector.

2. There's less distraction—no noise of film being run, no one working in sight of the audience.

3. The room need not be totally dark. Normal room lighting is acceptable, providing enough light for the group to take notes or follow printed instructions. (A lighted room will help keep your group awake. The darkened room is sleep-inducing, particularly if the meeting is held after the participants have worked eight hours and are tired.)

4. You have freedom of movement. You can walk in front of the screen to point out something, without casting a shadow or interfering with projection.

5. You can see the audience.

6. It gives an air of professionalism.

The disadvantages of the rear-screen projection method are:

1. More space is needed. You need sufficient room behind the screen to set up the projector and to throw the image. (You can shorten the throw by using a mirror, set up so that the projected beam hits the mirror at an angle and reflects on the screen at an angle. You may also use mirrors in this way with slides: put the slides into the projector backwards, and they will appear right-side up on the screen. Another way of getting a short throw is to use a wide-angle lens.)

   To show motion pictures by the rear-screen method, however, you must have sufficient room. Mirrors cannot be used, for the simple reason that motion-picture film does not make sense when it is run backwards. Furthermore, the sound track is on one side of the film only, which also prevents backward use of the film.

2. The area behind the screen must be masked or curtained.

3. A special rear-projection screen that is supported on its edges is needed. This isn't always available.

4. Rear-screen projection is more involved than front-screen.

Some rear-screen equipment is available for small audiences of 35 or less. There are cabinets especially designed for rear-screen projection; some are mounted on wheels and can easily be moved about. With them, you can use standard motion-picture, slide, or filmstrip projectors. Some are designed for specific projectors; others accommodate any model.

i) *Mock-ups and cut-away models*

Mock-ups and cut-away models of actual equipment are probably as close to realism as you can get. They are very useful if the real article is not available, or if you want to show its inner workings. These items usually permit you to give an effective working demonstration.

Although some mock-ups or models may be small enough to pass around for everyone to handle, it is better not to do so: those looking at the model will not pay attention to you, and may miss some important parts of your explanation. It is better to have a model for each person and to stop all other activity while the device is being examined—or, if there is but one model, to suggest that it be examined after the session.

The model or mock-up should not be shown until you are ready to refer to it. If it's large, it can be kept covered; if small, it can be kept under the lectern.

j) *Tape recorder*

Tape recorders are sometimes useful training aids. Their effectiveness depends upon the subject. You'll find them helpful if the participants will benefit from analyzing the presentations thus made.

However, attention spans are relatively short, and seven or eight minutes is about the longest attention span in this respect. You should, therefore, use the tape recorder only when you're certain you can do so effectively.

k) *Handouts*

Handouts (or passouts) are another communication aid. They are anything you distribute to the group, such as summaries, outlines, problems, case studies, and so forth.

Handouts should be accurate, neat, and attractive. You should, of course, have enough copies for everyone.

Never distribute handouts before you are ready to use them. A printed page is a temptation: some of the group will read it when they should be listening to you.

If you are going to use a simulated problem as the basis for group discussion, distribute the appropriate handout only when you are ready to discuss that problem. Do not attempt to continue talking while the materials are being distributed; no one will be listening.

Many handouts, such as summaries or outlines, should be distributed at the end of the session. Be sure to allow enough time for this to be done in an orderly way. Incidentally, in addition to giving the participants a summary, you're giving them the feeling of taking something with them.

1) *Video tape recorder*

One of the newest communication aids is the video tape recorder, which is really another name for closed-circuit television. This permits instant re-play of an event, a meeting, a speech, or what have you. An individual or group is taped while in action and the tape then played back, permitting the individual or group to see how he or they looked and sounded on TV. This playback provides "insightfulness" and enables an individual to see himself in an actual situation. The group or the instructor can point out what should be changed to make the presentation more effective, or what the good points were.

Video tape recording is especially effective for making a critique of an individual or a group. In many areas, equipment for this may be rented.

Communication aids are intended chiefly for the benefit of your class, but they are equally beneficial to you. The greatest benefit to you, the instructor, comes in preparing these aids, and analyzing your presentation and subject matter so that you can select the most effective ones.

Preparation of Communication Aids

There are seven basic rules to keep in mind when you prepare your communication aids (or have them prepared for you):

(a) The aid must be appropriate and relevant to your material. It should reinforce or demonstrate your main point or points. Also, it should illustrate only the points contained in your presentation—no others. One aid for each main point is a good "rule of thumb."

(b) The aid should be simple. A complicated aid detracts and confuses, while a simple one insures that the class sees the point you want to make. Also, a confusing or complex aid can be discouraging to the viewer. He doesn't want to take the time or effort to figure it out, so he ignores the whole thing.

(c) The aid must be accurate. An inaccurate aid reflects on your competence as an instructor, thus affecting the confidence the group has in you.

(d) The aid must be readable by everyone. An aid that cannot be read is worthless, disturbing, discouraging, and distracting.

(e) The aid must always be subordinate to your presentation. An aid must supplement, not take the place of, the presentation. It should not dominate the session, but be used as it is intended—to aid understanding and retention.

(f) The aid must be manageable. If an aid is to be effective, you must be able to use it without difficulty. You should be completely familiar with it and its operation. It should be constructed so that you'll have no problems with it, such as slides that don't focus, pages that won't turn, etc.

(g) The aid should be portable. Portability is not always a factor, true, but you will find that portable aids enable you to be much more flexible. You will not be restricted to one location—may not be available when you want it.

How to Use Communication Aids

There are definite techniques for effective use of specific communication aids; these we discussed when we talked about each aid. There are some general rules, however, for using communication aids that should be kept in mind.

(a) Be completely familiar with equipment and its use. Be certain you can operate or use the aid correctly and without problems. Practice using it until you are confident and at ease.

(b) Use only a few aids. Too many aids will be ineffective.

(c) Arrange aids so that everyone can see and/or hear. Get to the meeting place in sufficient time to set up your aids before the group convenes.

(d) Be certain the aid is functioning correctly.

(e) Don't let the aid dominate or in any other way interfere with your presentation.

(f) When possible, use a variety of aids. Adults respond best to a variety of teaching methods. (But see Point "b.")

(g) Use the aid at the proper time.

(h) Remove or turn off the communication aid after you have finished with it.

(i) Speak to the class, not to the aid.

Communication aids, properly used, add to any presentation. Incorrectly used, they are an annoyance and a distraction.

6

Methods of Teaching

The Lecture Method

The lecture is a very comon method of instruction, in which the leader or instructor does all of the talking. Lecturing is a relatively inefficient way of instruction because it does not actively involve the members of the group. It can be effective only if in some way the group can be induced to "think through" the information as it is being presented. This can be accomplished by having the individuals take notes, or the instructor can secure attention and hold interest by using communication aids.

Lectures may be used to introduce a new subject or topic. You can motivate as you introduce the subject, arousing interest as you set the stage for what is to come. A lecture does permit you to cover a great deal of material in the least amount of time —you have no interruptions, no questions, no discussion. It also enables you to go directly to your desired objective; you will not be diverted. When you have a large group, a lecture may be mandatory. A lecture can also be used as your summary at the end of a session.

In the lecture method, the individuals in the group play a passive role. There is no exchange of ideas, no participation, no practice. You appeal to the fewest senses, and you have little opportunity to evaluate the group reaction and adjust your material accordingly.

When you use the lecture method, start by motivating the individuals immediately. Make your introduction challenging and stimulating. Use language that is easy to understand—preferably short, accurate sentences. Use "you" and contractions ("don't," rather than "do not") to make your presentation conversational. Keep in mind that your main purpose is to communicate ideas to others.

The Discussion Method

The discussion method may also be described as the conference or seminar method. In it the members of the group and you, the leader, take part in a discussion and an exchange of ideas and information. You, as the instructor, steer the group toward a predetermined objective. Group participation is the hallmark of the discussion method.

This method stimulates thinking by involving the individual members of the group. It is usually done on an informal basis, which is conducive to learning and retention. It can be quite interesting and informative, if properly conducted.

The discussion method is, however, more time-consuming than the lecture. It is most adaptable to a small group—twenty-five or fewer. In a large group, usually only a few participate; shy or reticent individuals remain quiet.

The discussion method demands that you control the group very subtly. You have to be alert and constantly on your toes. You also should have a good background in the subject, and be able to question skillfully.

The discussion method can be used to resolve problems after a lecture, after a film has been shown, or after a demonstration.

The Demonstration-Performance Method

The demonstration-performance method combines an actual portrayal of procedures or operations with practice by the individual. In this method, the individual is told what to do and shown how to do it, and then given an opportunity to do it. It's a tell-show-do method, which might be described as an acted-out lecture.

A well-planned demonstration, skillfully executed, is very effective. In this method, you appeal to all the senses; provide actual practice; stimulate interest; and maintain attention.

This method is effective for groups of twenty-five or less. It is not, however, practical for a large group, unless you can divide the group into small segments for the practice part, with an instructor or leader for each segment.

Planning for a demonstration requires that you break the skill or activity into various steps, arranged in logical order. You must become completely familiar with these steps, and practice

so you can make a skillful, effective demonstration. You have to arrange also for equipment, if any, and for the individuals to practice. Considerable time will be used for individual performances, so you must consider this in arranging the session. A summary or review should be made after everyone has had the opportunity to practice.

By careful observation during the performance part, you can spot—and remedy—incorrect techniques in the beginning before they become established habit patterns.

Dramatization Method

Participation and interest on the part of the group can be increased by using dramatization. This is actually a combination of demonstration and discussion, with individuals from the group doing the demonstrating. To a certain extent, dramatization is unplanned demonstration. Certain guidelines, however, must be provided for the individuals taking part.

Dramatization involves the acting out by individuals, without script or rehearsal, of job techniques needed in specific situations. The participants are told by the instructor what the situation and desired outcome are and, in general terms, how each actor should move toward accomplishing the desired outcome.

You can use dramatization to stimulate the group to take a new look at familiar job techniques; or it can be used to help the group develop the confidence and skills needed for techniques that are new to them.

You can use dramatization if:

(a) The individuals in the group are completely at ease with one another and with you.

(b) A friendly, cooperative atmosphere exists, so that no one will ridicule the actors or "ham up" the acting.

(c) A number of individuals are willing to participate without rehearsal.

(d) You are completely familiar with the technique. You must be prepared for the possibility of an individual becoming embarrassed or upset.

The procedure for dramatization consists of the following steps:

(a) Describe the situation to be dramatized and the desired outcome. Make this as clear as possible.

(b) Ask for volunteers for the parts, or select individuals to portray the roles. Do not force anyone to take part.

(c) Allow the actors a few minutes to discuss in a general way what they want to do. While they are doing this, tell the others what to watch for. Ask the audience to withhold their comments until the end of the dramatization.

(d) When the important points have been sufficiently portrayed to provide a basis for discussion, stop the dramatization. Do this even if the desired outcome has not been reached.

(e) After the dramatization, conduct a discussion of it. Explore with the group the reason why the action took the direction that it did. You might ask: Was the desired result achieved (or about to be achieved)? How did each actor's behavior influence the result?

As the discussion is taking place, you can bring in those points that you want covered. You can also help the group relate the dramatization to similar real job situations.

Business Games (Simulation)

Business games have become a popular teaching technique in recent years. It is a method used primarily for management training, and in many management-development programs one or more such games are included. The method has been adopted also by forward-looking business educators as an exciting and promising new approach to college training for business administration students.

While simulation is fairly new to training in business, it has been used extensively for years by the military. War games, field maneuvers, and map exercises have proved invaluable to the training of officers and staffs, as exercises in the strategy, planning, and decision-making these men will be expected to apply in actual situations later in their careers.

Business games are similar. They are simulation exercises where the participants have an opportunity to perform under conditions that closely match on-the-job atmosphere. (In some ways, it is similar to the role-playing method discussed below.) The participants play roles such as Marketing Manager, Controller, President, etc. However, where a role-playing exercise is tightly structured, with a narrow margin of deviation from the script, business games are purposely structured so that the participants can decide their own courses of action in various situations and in relation to various problems presented throughout the game.

Games may be designed so that all trainees play the same role, thus competing against every other trainee. Or, they may be designed so that trainees are organized into teams, representing hypothetical companies in mutual competition. In either situation, participants receive extensive training in business strategy, analysis of business reports and information, planning, and decision-making.

As in any other method, there are advantages and disadvantages associated with business games. Some of the advantages are:

1. The players become deeply involved in the game and thus motivation for learning is at a high level. The spirit of competition also motivates trainees to more active participation than would be the case in most other methods.

2. Games are dynamic, moving situations, where the trainee takes action and then gets feedback to see the results of his action.

3. In game situations, several interacting variables must be simultaneously weighed in decisions by the player. Since this is approximately the case in daily business activities, it gives the player a better appreciation for the difficulty of making decisions, plus practice in the process.

4. The player gains knowledge of and practice in the use of tools that assist in decision making. He sees the function served by reports, charts, studies, etc., and learns how to analyze, appraise, and apply such information.

Some of the disadvantages are:

1. Some games require the use of coaching or "umpire" personnel in addition to the instructor.

2. More planning and development is required than with a simple role-playing or case-study exercise.

3. With sophisticated games, computers or other expensive and elaborate equipment may be necessary.

4. Because games usually involve relatively larger blocks of time than other methods, there is a tendency to impose unrealistic time factors on some of the operations to be performed by players. Players quickly recognize these time pressures and tend to excuse or at least discount poor performance on their part.

For an examination of Management Games in more detail than can be offered here, the interested reader is referred to the extensive literature on the subject.

Role Play

Role play is similar to dramatization. In fact, the two are often confused. However, a crucial difference is that in role

64

play the leader does not determine the outcome in advance. He tells the actors how they "feel," and each actor tries to behave according to these feelings. The emotion of the actors determines the outcome of role play. Role play, therefore, is used to help understand human behavior and improve those skills involved in working with people.

The conditions for using role play are the same as for dramatization. There must be friendly atmosphere, individuals must be at ease with each other, and the leader must be familiar with the role-play technique. Since emotions are involved and, moreover, are likely to be portrayed vividly, there is always the possibility that some of the actors or the audience will become "overinvolved." The leader must be prepared to resolve any resulting emotional problems in the discussion period that follows.

The procedure for using role play is:

(a) Select a situation that will be meaningful to the group. If this is the first time role playing has been used, select a situation that does not involve the specific job responsibilities of anyone in the group. This will permit the participants to be more objective in their observations and analysis. In the more detached atmosphere of the discussion period, you can help the individuals relate the situation to their own jobs.

(b) Ask individuals to volunteer for the role play.

(c) Give written instructions to each player. These should indicate, in detail, whom he is to portray, the "mood" he is to be in, and how he feels at the beginning. Remind the actors that they should act as the kind of people they are supposed to be. Allow the actors a few minutes to adjust to the mood of their roles—individually, not as a group.

(d) While the actors are doing this, tell the others what the situation is. If you want to, you may tell them what emotions are to be portrayed. Let the group know what to watch for. Also, remind the group that the actors are not portraying their own emotions but the emotions appropriate to their roles.

(e) Stop the role playing when real feelings begin to develop among the players—usually within three to seven minutes.

(f) Let the players tell why they behaved as they did, and how they felt about the behavior of the others involved in the role play. (The audience should again be reminded that the actors are discussing the emotions of the people they portrayed, not their own personal feelings.)

(g) In conducting a discussion, pattern your questions along the following lines:

(1) Did any actor suddenly change behavior? Why do you think this occurred?

(2) Did the actors seem to develop an understanding of each other? Why?

(3) What do you think the outcome would have been?

(4) Could the actors have improved their relationship? How?

(h) After a discussion of the specific events that took place, encourage the group to relate the events to their jobs.

Your role as instructor is very important in role play, because you have to be alert to emotional problems that can develop and to disturbing influences that may affect actors and audience. By skillfully handling the discussion, you can preserve each individual's dignity.

Buzz Groups

Buzz groups are small gatherings (three to six individuals, usually) formed to work out a relatively uncomplicated problem during a brief informal session. Usually the groups work by themselves, although the instructor is available if needed. Buzz groups are not appropriate for presenting new material, being better suited to finding out how well familiar material is understood or what individuals think about a particular subject.

To use the buzz-group technique, you must first divide your large group into smaller groups of from three to six people. You may either appoint a chairman and recorder or ask each group to select its own; or, this leadership may be permitted to arise spontaneously from within the group.

Next, you should explain clearly what each group is to do. These instructions may be distributed in typewritten form or given orally. Each group may get the same assignment or each group may be given a different assignment, concerned with different aspects of the same topic.

You should watch each group as it works and be available for any assistance it may need.

When most of the groups have completed their tasks, bring the groups together. The recorder of each group is called upon to give a concise report of the conclusions of his group. You can then conduct a discussion based on these results.

In-Basket Method

The in-basket method has proved to be an effective technique for training management personnel in problem-solving and decision-making. The technique is also adaptable to some other specific training situations, such as the training of correspondents.

The method consists of presenting to the participants materials and problems representing a cross-section of items that might normally cross their desks for action. The trainee decides how he will handle each item and makes a record of the action taken. Normally, there will be differences in action by the various members of the group. After one or more items have been handled, the group discusses the different responses. Through this group discussion, the principles of management or supervision are developed in a very meaningful way. Proponents feel strongly that principles are better taught and reinforced by this method than by the lecture method used alone.

Many variations of this method are possible. An in-basket exercise may be just one part of one session in a training program—or it may be comprehensive enough to be central to the total program. An exercise may be used to test the knowledge gained by the participants in a training program; it can also be used for the training of persons who can meet only occasionally (or not at all), because they work at different times and/or locations. Under these conditions, materials are sent to the trainees. They prepare a report of the action they would take on each item and return this report to the instructor. If the group can meet occasionally, discussion is conducted at that time. If the group can never meet, the instructor prepares a critique of each trainee's handling and sends it to him.

With careful planning and organization; through utilizing materials that are pertinent; and by making sure that all communications are at a reading and understanding level appropriate to the trainees, very effective training can be accomplished through the in-basket method.

The Use of Problem Situations or Case Studies

Presenting a problem situation or a case study gives the participants an opportunity to apply new knowledge to specific situations. It stimulates discussion and participation.

To construct a case study, you should follow certain guidelines. First, the problem or case study should be so constructed that it is realistic (as far as the participants are concerned). They should be able to recognize it as relevant to them and their jobs.

The statement of the problem (or the premise of the case study) should be brief and simply worded, though complete enough to be understood. It can be made believable by including "statements" of individuals involved in the problem: these will be used to reveal attitudes and feelings. The problem or case study should be one that involves decision and action, and should also suggest complex problems which are not immediately evident. Finally, there should be definite instructions as to what is to be done—usually in the form of questions to be answered by the participants.

It's good to distribute a copy of the case study or problem to each individual so that he can refer to it as necessary.

The individuals should be given time to work on the problem and arrive at a solution. Then a discussion should be conducted. The purpose of the discussion is to help the individuals use problem-solving techniques.

You should guide the individuals to consider each of the following steps:

a) Look for the real problem. By getting answers to questions such as who, what, when, where, and why, you can pinpoint the problem and its causes.

b) Gather all the *facts*. (Guesswork and mere opinion are irrelevant.)

c) Evaluate the facts.

d) Develop possible solutions.

e) Select the best solution and apply it.

Although all of these steps may not apply to a particular problem or case study, the individuals should be made aware of them.

On-The-Job Training (O.J.T.)

Most of the training methods discussed up to this point have involved *group* instruction; however, there are instances when the ratio of one trainee to one instructor is desirable, with training taking place at the trainee's regular workplace in a production climate. This method of instruction is known as On-The-Job Training.

In this training method, the individual doing the instructing is either the trainee's supervisor, or someone under the latter's jurisdiction to whom he has delegated the task—usually, one of his highest skilled employees, and one who, ideally, is also a reasonably effective instructor. In either case, the person instructing normally continues to perform his regular duties in addition to teaching the new employee. Production is not inter-rupted; on the contrary, the trainee contributes increasingly to production as his training advances. Initially, he is trained to perform some of the simple operations involved in the job. As training continues and his skill is further developed, the trainee learns more advanced operations. He keeps adding to his range of skills until, ultimately, he can perform the entire operation.

O.J.T. involves the transmitting of a well-defined skill from one person who possesses it to another who does not. As in other training methods, O.J.T. is founded on the principles of learning discussed earlier in this text. The individual doing the training must keep these principles in mind and apply them when conducting the training.

The advantages of the O.J.T. method include:

(1) The trainee learns by doing.

(2) The trainee learns in the actual work situation, under actual working conditions of the particular job, while he gains practical experience in the duties connected with that job.

(3) The trainee performs the operations over and over, thus reinforcing his learning through repetition.

(4) The trainee is able to gauge his own progress.

(5) The trainee's performance and progress are continually under review "on the spot" by the person doing the instructing.

As with all training methods, O.J.T. has some disadvantages. One of these is the fact that the trainee sometimes becomes frightened or overwhelmed by what appears to be an impossible learing task. He sees the complexities of the total job before he has learned the fundamentals, and—unless he can relate this to his state of training—the final job may look discouragingly difficult.

Since this method includes productive effort along with training, another disadvantage is that the training activity is extended over a longer period of time than is the case with other training techniques. Also, the company must accept the risk that some of the trainee's mistakes may affect the quality of the product units on which he worked. And finally, the fact that the method usually involves one instructor and one trainee may be considered a disadvantage, since only a limited number of individuals can be trained at one time.

There are five steps to be performed by the trainer if O.J.T. is to be effective. These are:

1. Prepare to instruct.

2. Prepare the trainee for instruction.

3. Present the operation to the trainee.

4. Have the trainee perform each part of the operation as it is taught.

5. Follow up on the training, make corrections, and reinforce.

It is of the utmost importance that the trainer understand the value of each of these five steps, and the role they play in meeting the final training objective.

In preparing to instruct, the trainer must:

1. Break down the job into its several elements. This involves writing down, in order, all the points that will be taught and demonstrated to the employee. To the extent possible, the elements of the job should be taught in the same sequence as the final job is performed. At the same time, the trainee must be taken from the simple to the complex operation and from the known to the unknown.

2. Prepare a timetable within which the various elements will be taught. The trainer must decide how much the trainee can reasonably be expected to learn in a certain period of time. This timetable is used to gauge the trainee's development.

3. Prepare the work area where the training will take place. It is the instructor's responsibility to be sure that the proper tools, equipment, and materials necessary for instruction are readily available and in working condition. Safety devices must be checked to insure that they function correctly. The area should be set up just as the trainee is expected to maintain it, from an organization and housekeeping standpoint.

Obviously, if this first step is to be performed effectively, a lesson plan (or plan of action) is required. The type of plan selected depends on the trainer and what he needs to accomplish, as well as on the depth of training experience that he brings to the job.

In preparing the trainee for instruction, the trainer needs to put the trainee at ease and, in addition, to determine what he already knows about the job and about the tools and equipment he will use in performing it. Some of the instruction may be by-passed if the trainee's knowledge warrants it. The instructor must also motivate and encourage the trainee to do his best, so that his interest in learning the job will be high.

In presenting the operation, the trainer is required to do the following:

1. Explain and demonstrate the operation carefully and patiently.

2. Stress key points (and continue to reinforce them frequently).

3. After teaching one element of the job, ask questions and have the employee demonstrate his familiarity with that element before going on to the next.

4. Be careful not to exceed an amount of instruction beyond what the employee can grasp and master at one time.

The trainer must test the trainee's performance frequently. This should include the following steps:

1. Have the trainee perform the job or parts of it under close observation.

2. Have the employee explain each element and show how it is performed.

3. Correct any errors made by the trainee and reinforce the correct method.

The trainer is now ready to put the trainee on his own. Before doing so, however, he must inform the trainee where he can go for help. He must also continue to follow up with inspections and checks of the trainee's work, until he is sure that the trainee can perform and is performing the tasks correctly, under only normal supervision.

Vestibule Method of Training

The Vestibule Method of training derives its name from the old vestibule school in industry—a department in an industrial establishment where new employees were trained for the work they would do on a regular job. The school was separate from production facilities, its only function being to train new employees in the performance of a certain job *before* they were actually assigned to one of the regular production or operating departments of the company.

This was a fairly popular method of training more than two decades ago (notably, during World War II). At this time, the major defense industries had an immediate and pressing need to train large numbers of employees simultaneously for one specific operation, such as welding or riveting. The Vestibule Method was ideal under these circumstances: one instructor could train eight or ten persons at a time, and, after devoting their full time to training, these trainees could be introduced into the production line within a few weeks.

At the same time, however, this method was expensive: the company had to maintain a staff of full-time instructors; production-line equipment had to be duplicated in the classroom; during the period of training, wages were paid to the trainee without any return in production; and, finally, materials worked on by the trainees became scrap, which contributed nothing to the end product of the company. Consequently, the company had to absorb the expense involved as a pure training cost. These employees contributed nothing to the productive efforts of the company until after their training was completed, at which time they were placed on a regular production-line job.

After World War II, the method lost its popularity. The reasons are obvious: companies no longer needed to train as many people, and were no longer willing to absorb the extra expense involved in this training method. They reverted to other methods more in tune with their needs and involving training costs they were willing to accept.

Vestibule training is similar to on-the-job training in one respect. The five functions required of the instructor are the same. He must:

(1) Prepare to instruct.

(2) Prepare the trainee for instruction.

(3) Present the operation to the trainee.

(4) Have the trainee perform each part of the operation as it is taught.

(5) Follow up on the training, make corrections, and reinforce.

From this point on, however, the differences are pronounced, and include the following:

(1) The trainer is a full-time instructor, rather than a line supervisor or fellow worker.

(2) Vestibule training seldom uses a one-to-one, trainer-trainee ratio. The instructor teaches several persons at one time, depending upon the number of employees needed and on the sophistication of the skill being communicated.

(3) This training takes place apart from the actual work area. The trainees learn the needed skill prior to their assignment to the production line.

As indicated previously, there are several disadvantages to this method.

(1) The added expense of professional instructors whose entire time is spent on training.

(2) The devotion of space, equipment, and materials strictly to training.

(3) Payment of wages to trainees for a period of time during which they contribute nothing to the productive efforts of the company.

Vestibule training has regained some of its former popularity in the "hard-core" and minority-group training programs established in recent years. Because the method concentrates on the development of a skill before entering the production area, results with these groups have been better than when an alternate training method has been used.

The Selection of Method

You, as the instructor, should select the training method to be used. No one method is best. The ideal is a combination of all three: lecture, discussion, and performance. Many factors will influence your decision, such as the nature of the subject; overall objectives; group size; time and facilities available; and so forth.

A combination of training methods will provide a change of pace and help maintain interest. It will help you emphasize the different facets of a subject, and make your sessions more stimulating and effective.

7

Conduct of the Instructor

Responsibility

As an instructor, much of the responsibility for the success of the program rests on you. You are in charge, and how you conduct each session will have a great influence on how the participants respond. You can instill interest and motivate the group—or you can distract and bore them, causing them to lose interest. It is your responsibility to motivate, to instill enthusiasm, and to impart knowledge, skills, and proper attitudes to the group.

Preparation

You must be thoroughly prepared to present a topic. This means research—getting a good background in the subject, increasing your own knowledge of it. It means making lesson plans, and it means practice. A practice session can be very helpful in enabling you to make an effective presentation, to "get rid of the bugs." It will help you check your material and enable you to become familiar with your communication aids and perfect your timing. For every hour of actual instruction, you should invest a minimum of three hours in preparation.

This preparation should include getting everything ready for the session: the room arranged for maximum comfort and best visibility; communication aids set up in operating order, in such a way that they can be seen and heard by everyone. Check these things yourself, and don't wait until the last minute to do so: you may need an extension cord, a light bulb, chalk, or other equipment. To delay a session while such items are obtained reflects unfavorably on your efficiency as an instructor. Sometimes such a delay is unavoidable, but this should be the rare exception.

Punctuality

Sessions should start on time. If individuals have to wait, their interest wanes. They begin to feel that the leader is indifferent—that he doesn't attach much importance to the session—so why should they?

Everyone attending your sessions should be made aware of the value of classroom time. You have a given amount of material to cover and a specified time in which to do it. Either the individual himself or the company he works for has paid for the course and is entitled to the maximum benefits. This can be accomplished only by having everyone in his seat, ready to go at the appointed hour. You will have to maintain tight discipline in this area if your program is to be a success.

It is just as important to end on time. If you're scheduled to end at 10:00 o'clock, it's better to end two minutes early than five minutes late. Regardless of how interesting a program may be, the participants will start to get restless if you run overtime. It can upset their schedule and they become understandably concerned. Under these circumstances, they aren't apt to be very attentive. It's also a reflection on your ability for planning and on your ability to keep the program on schedule.

Break Time

If classes are scheduled to run longer than two hours, you should tell the group they will have a break. In an all-day session, it is common practice to allow one fifteen-minute break in the morning and another in the afternoon. These rest periods are extremely valuable and should not be ignored: those in attendance become far less receptive and attentive if break time is delayed. Remind the class to report back promptly at the end of all breaks. It is your responsibility, as instructor, to resume class promptly at the end of break time.

Rest Rooms

Frequently those in attendance will be unfamiliar with the building where the sessions are held. This is particularly true if your program is being held at a public establishment, such as a motel or hotel. The location of rest rooms should be pointed out during your opening remarks, with a reminder at break time during the first session.

Telephone Messages

Make arrangements to have all telephone messages held until just before break time. The switchboard operator should have a copy of your schedule, so that she can send all messages in written form to you for distribution. Inform the group of these arrangements and stress that those wishing to return phone calls should do so during the allotted break time and not wait until after they have had coffee. Here is an area in which you will have to maintain strict control, as interruptions can become quite distracting.

Assignments

Home-work assignments should be collected at the beginning of the session. If students are permitted to keep their papers and turn them in at the end of the session, some will always make use of session time to complete the assignment. Make it clear that late assignments either will not be accepted or will be accepted with a penalty.

No program can be very successful unless order and discipline are maintained. And it is your responsibility as leader to lay the ground rules for your program during your opening remarks.

Dress

The instructor who is not appropriately dressed handicaps himself. To command the respect of the group, you should look and act like an instructor. Remember, you are setting an example—you are the model. Your neat appearance indicates a respect for yourself and for the group.

Get Attention

You should not start the session until you have everyone's attention. Usually this is not difficult—often, simply walking to the lectern will cause the group to become quiet. Sometimes it will be necessary to ask for their attention, but a simple "Good evening" (or whatever is appropriate) will customarily produce the desired results.

Speak In A Friendly Tone

Use a conversational tone—don't orate or declaim. Maintain attention by occasionally varying your tone and rate of speaking. You can transmit friendliness by your tone, and also by utilizing the word "you." You identify with the group when you say "you and I" and "we." If you can establish the impression that you and the group are working in a common cause, you will gain the desired rapport.

Establish Eye Contact

When you talk to a friend, you look at him, don't you? For much the same reason, you should look at your group, too. This will help establish a friendly atmosphere; also, it will help you to be alert to the group—to know what is going on. You can use eye contact for effective control—to keep everyone with you—and to determine whether or not you are understood.

You establish eye contact by letting your eyes roam over the group. Gaze directly into the eyes of each person for just a fraction of a second. In other words, allow your eyes to make contact with those in the group. Be careful that you do not concentrate your gaze on one person or one section of the group. If you do, others will lose interest.

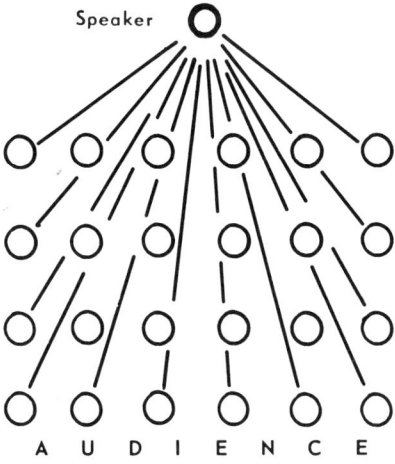

Speaker

A U D I E N C E

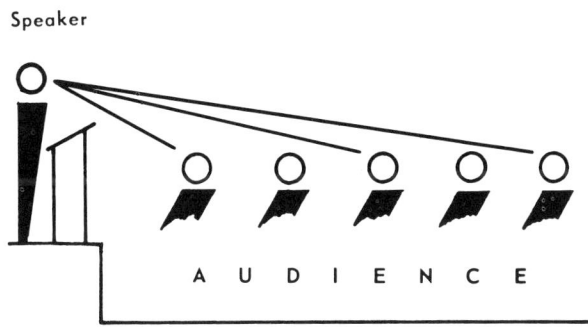

Speaker

A U D I E N C E

Watch Your Posture

You should stand comfortably straight. Do not lean on the lectern or speaker's stand—it detracts from your effectiveness. You can rest your hands on the lectern, but don't use it as a support: don't get a "death grip" on it.

The quality of your voice is also affected by posture. When you slump, your lungs and diaphragm are constricted and your voice distorted. Voice distortion will occur, too, if you tilt your head to look down at your notes. (This also destroys eye contact.) Stand about six inches back from the lectern, to avoid having to lower your head to look at your notes: that way, you can simply drop your eyes to your notes. This will also help you avoid leaning on the lectern.

Speak to Be Understood

If you are to be understood, you must first be heard. Speak loudly enough—if someone can't hear you, or has to strain to hear you, he will lose interest. You can gauge the proper volume of your voice to the size of the room and the conditions under which you are speaking. Use a microphone or loudspeaker system, when necessary. This is easier on you and on your audience. Remember to adjust the microphone ahead of time, and, if you have never used one before, to practice with it. You should be able to use your normal speaking voice if the amplifying system is properly adjusted.

Pronunciation is important, too, if you want to be understood. Use words that are familiar to you—words you know you can pronounce correctly. Also enunciate carefully: don't slur sounds and words together. Your aim is to use speech that is clear and understandable.

Use Gestures

You should use gestures only if they are natural. A stilted or forced gesture does not add to your presentation; it detracts. Of course, you don't want to be immobile or expressionless; you

WRONG

WRONG

WRONG

RIGHT

83

want to be conversational. As you become involved in your subject and its presentation, you'll discover that your movements and gestures come naturally. Using communication aids will also help you to move naturally. Avoid extremes of movement, such as pacing or standing rigidly in one spot. Your aim is for relaxed, natural movements.

Avoid Distracting Mannerisms

Any mannerism which takes the group's attention away from the subject is distracting. You should avoid doing such things as rattling change or keys in a pocket; toying with pointer, chalk, or pencil; tugging at a necktie; stroking your throat, ear, or hair; or rocking back and forth.

Control Nervousness

Nervousness is normal, and even the most experienced speakers and instructors experience it. It is nature's way of preparing you to meet a challenge. Faced with a challenge, your body prepares to meet it: your adrenalin flows, your heartbeat increases, and your respiration changes. If the challenge involves physical activity, this extra energy created would be burned off, and the body would return to normal after the challenge had been met. Since physical activity is not ordinarily involved in a training session, the adrenalin has nothing to do, so it becomes "butterflies" in your stomach. This is actually a sign that you're ready to meet the challenge.

Experience doesn't eliminate the "butterflies." In fact, many individuals have found that when they do *not* have this uneasy feeling, they do not do as well. However, experience will help you to control this nervousness and use it to your advantage. But how do you control it?

First of all, be thoroughly prepared. If you're confident that you know your subject, and know how to present it effectively, you'll have more confidence. Know your opening remarks very well—the first few minutes are the test. Once you have successfully passed that test, you settle down and the session goes well.

It's also important to have the proper mental attitude. Keep in mind that the group is there to learn from you, and that they are more interested in the subject than they are in you personally. One reason for nervousness is your understandable concern about the group's acceptance of you and of what you present. If you are thoroughly prepared and have something solid to present, you need not be concerned about an adverse reaction.

Be deliberate. Nervousness may cause you to talk faster than normal, so make an effort to talk more slowly at the start. Concentrate on this, and you will soon find that you are speaking normally.

Concentrate on helping the group to relax. They are anxious and apprehensive, too. If you tell them a story, for example, you will find that you will forget about your own feelings. You'll relax along with the group. (Be certain, of course, that the story is relevant to the subject, and in good taste.)

Remember that the group is listening to you "one at a time." Think in terms of one individual at a time to eliminate your nervousness at facing a group.

Don't Apologize

You should approach each session with a positive attitude. The group is expecting the best from you—and it is entitled to no less. Don't do or say anything which will convey that you are unprepared, or uninformed, or unable to present the material. Such excuses will only undermine the group's confidence in you and call attention to weaknesses which might otherwise have gone unnoticed.

Be Poised

You must be in control of yourself at all times. You cannot allow yourself to become irritated or upset. You'll need to be amenable to change, to be flexible. You should be receptive to constructive criticism and able to adjust your presentation as necessary.

Be Enthusiastic

You must be enthusiastic about your subject and the program. If you aren't, the group won't be either. If you want to motivate and inspire, you should display enthusiasm. You do this by the interest you take in your role as an instructor. Your care in preparation; your skill in presenting the material; and the interest you show will create a contagious enthusiasm among the participants. As Henry Ford said of enthusiasm: "With it there is accomplishment. Without it there are only alibis."

8

Motivation and Control of the Group

Motivation

Motivation—inspiring the participants to learn—is basic to any successful training session. No matter how well prepared you may be, if the individuals are not receptive to your presentation there will be little or no learning. You'll recall that "Adults learn when they want to learn." As an instructor you can do much to encourage learning. You can instill in the participants a desire to learn and to participate in the session.

In your preparation, you considered motivation and made it part of your plan. You incorporated it into the introduction, body, and summary of the plan. This is necessary: you must constantly work at getting and maintaining interest.

How you start the session and how you conduct it are elements of motivation. You should conduct each session in a friendly, sincere manner. Your attitude should be one of *wanting* to share experiences and ideas. To do this, you must be understood by each person in your group—and you must attempt to understand him.

The physical setup of your meeting place will influence the attitude of the participants. It is not always possible to have ideal meeting conditions, but you should strive to make them as good as possible. You'll find that a V-shape, a T-shape, or a U-shape arrangement works well. Chairs should be comfortable, and arranged so that everyone can see and hear easily. Everyone should have a place to write. The room should be well-lighted, adequately ventilated, and at a proper temperature. Ash trays and drinking water should be provided. Set the room up to be as free from distractions as possible. (Everyone, of course, should be informed of the meeting place and the time.)

At the first session, introduce yourself. Then, if the participants do not know each other, ask each one to state his name, position, and where he works. (You can vary this information, depending on the group.) In some sessions, you might want a brief indication of what each one expects to get from the session. This information is helpful to you. You may wish to slant the material to the wants of the group.

It's a good idea to have name cards on which the individual writes his name, after which he places the card in front of him. This helps the participants get acquainted. A card such as the one shown in Fig. 14 permits the name to be visible to both the participants and the conference leader. If the participants use a grease crayon and write large, you will be able to see it easily. It is not always necessary to include title and name of company on the name card.

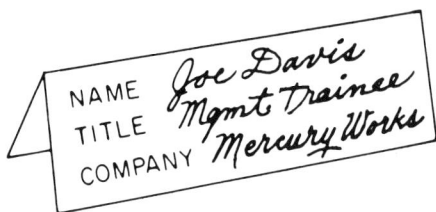

NAME *Joe Davis*
TITLE *Mgmt Trainee*
COMPANY *Mercury Works*

NOTE: Card should contain same information on both sides

FIGURE 14.

After the introductions have been made, you should introduce the topic and tell how the session is going to be conducted. If you're going to have a break or breaks, let the group know. At this point you want to encourage participation. Let the group know that questions, comments, and ideas are welcome. Make them feel that this is *their* program. Let them know how the sessions are going to benefit them, how the topic relates to them, what the objectives are.

Be natural, sincere, and honest with the group. In so doing, you'll gain their respect. Have a positive, enthusiastic attitude toward the group. Don't be negative; don't be apologetic. You should not make any excuses or indicate in any way that you aren't prepared or qualified to present the material. If you've done your research and prepared for the session, no apology is needed.

As the session develops and you begin to get participation from the group, utilize the contributions. Make everyone feel important. Comments such as "That's a good point" and "As you said, Mr. Jones" will encourage the group. Use the names of individuals whenever possible.

Control of the Group

Your group will be made up of individuals, each one different from the others, but, primarily, they'll act and respond as a group. However, since you're encouraging participation, the personalities of the individuals will show and you must deal with them. For example, one person may try to do all the talking, while another will not contribute anything. You will have to know how to handle these different types tactfully, so that you won't have a "mental dropout"—or a physical one! To do this, you need to know something about the causes of different reactions from members of the group, and something about what you can do to prevent or modify the reaction.

The Silent Individual

Some of the causes for silence on the part of an individual are:

a) He may not be interested in the subject or topic. He has not been motivated—he can't see the value of the session for him.

b) He may be uncertain or confused. Perhaps the objectives aren't clear to him. Perhaps he does not understand the previous discussions.

c) He may think that he doesn't have sufficient background or knowledge to make a contribution. He may prefer to keep quiet rather than to appear foolish in front of the others.

d) He may feel that he doesn't belong to the group.

e) He may be a slow thinker. Many times an individual will be thinking about something and preparing to express an idea on it, but before he is ready to do so, someone else says it for him.

f) He may simply prefer to listen.

You're probably already thinking of some preventive measures that you can take. For one thing, you can be certain that everyone is informed as to the subject and the objectives. You can relate the subject to the group's needs, making it as personal as possible. You can—indeed, you must—create a friendly atmosphere.

During the session, you can help the individual contribute. If you're alert to the people in your group, you'll sense when someone wants to contribute. His expression will give you a clue. You can then comment, "John, you look as if you want to say something." (If John shakes his head negatively, don't press the issue.)

You can ask a relay-type question—one that each person in the group answers in turn. By including a timid person in this series of around-the-horn comments, you help him "break the ice."

Although "yes or no" questions are not desirable, you might make an exception and direct one to the silent person to help him say something.

To insure understanding and to aid the slow thinker, frequent summarization is good.

The Monopolizer

The monopolizer is the opposite of the silent person. He talks so much no one else has a chance. He may try to monopolize the session because:

a) He has knowledge that others do not have.

b) He wants to be helpful and share his ideas and experiences with the group.

c) He may be so enthusiastic that he becomes impatient with the "slow" pace and tries to speed up the group's progress.

d) He may be a "know-it-all."

e) He may want to assert himself as the leader of the group.

f) He may want recognition from the group and the instructor.

If, at the beginning of the session, you make it clear that everyone is going to have an opportunity to participate, the individual who might otherwise become the monopolizer may not have the opportunity to become one. Others will contribute, and will also often let the monopolizer know that he is talking too much. If you know something about the individuals in the group before the session, you can plan on how to utilize each one's experience or ability.

During the session, you can ask the monopolizer to summarize. A comment such as, "I wonder if you would summarize all this for us, John," should result in his bringing his comments to a conclusion. You can then ask if there are any reactions from the others.

You can suggest that others express their opinions by saying, "You've been giving us a lot of good ideas, John. I'd like to hear from some of the others." Then direct a question to another individual in the group.

You can also repeat what you think his idea is, ask him if that is what he meant, and then ask for reactions from the others. You might say, "I'd like to be certain I understand your point. Is this what you mean?" Then state the idea in your words. If he agrees, then ask the other members of the group for their opinions.

The Side Tracker

An individual may attempt to steer the discussion in a direction away from the announced subject. This can happen because:

a) He doesn't understand the objectives of the session.

b) He wants to avoid the topic.

c) He has emotional problems which prevent him from concentrating on the subject.

d) He wants information not related to the topic.

You should make the objectives as clear as possible. You should let the group know at the very beginning the directions the session will take, and, in general, what will be covered. They will then know whether or not their questions will be answered during the program. They will also be in a position to weigh, in advance, whether or not their comments are pertinent. Perhaps something can be done to help the individual eliminate the emotional problem. If possible, find out why the person wants to avoid the subject and act accordingly.

During the session, you should try to relate what is said to the topic—particularly if there is a misunderstanding of the objectives. In some instances, you may have to rule directly that an idea or comment is not relevant, and bring the group back to the original topic. Do this as tactfully as you can. You may offer to discuss it later, or suggest that this be a topic for a future session.

Periods of Silence

Occasionally everyone in the group may fall silent. This may be caused by:

a) Boredom.

b) Fatigue from too long a session.

c) The fact that the group is thinking.

d) One individual who has impressed the group with his "expertness," making everyone else reluctant to speak.

e) Improper handling of group contributions by the instructor. You may have been too critical or too indifferent, or have ignored contributions.

f) The fact that the group doesn't want to be there.

How you start the session and your attitude throughout it can do much to avoid awkward periods of silence. The better job you do of developing interest and establishing a friendly atmosphere, the better participation will be. If the group is hostile toward the session or toward you, your task of motivation will be that much more difficult. You'll have to work harder; you'll have to be patient with the group. The more surely you show that the session will benefit the group, the quicker you'll overcome negative attitudes.

If you ask the group to think about something, give them sufficient time to do so. Remember that you are familiar with the problem or question, and presumably know the solution or answer, but this may be the first time the group has been confronted with it. It may seem to you that you are waiting a long time for the group to comment, but usually this is not the case.

Side Conversations During Sessions

Side conversations between two individuals occur because:

a) The individuals have no interest in the subject.

b) The presentation is uninteresting.

c) The group is tired.

d) The announced schedule is not being adhered to. (If you indicated a break at a certain time, and you do not stop at that time, individuals in the group will start checking with each other: "Aren't we supposed to have a break?" If the class runs overtime, you'll find the students saying, "We're supposed to quit at 10:00 o'clock. I have to go.")

e) An individual may not be certain he's right on some point, so he checks with the person next to him.

Again, the atmosphere you have established will help to eliminate side conversations. If individuals think they can express their opinion without censure, they are more likely to do so.

Adhering to the schedule will also help. This need not be strict adherence—a minute or two difference won't matter—but you shouldn't go too far overtime. If you find that you need more time, check with the group about what they want to do.

If a side conversation lasts only a minute or so, it can be ignored unless it is bothering the group. If the conversation continues, you can stop the session and wait for it to stop. Quite often the others in the group will handle this situation for you—they will silence the individuals.

As you can see, an instructor needs to understand people. The more you try to understand the individuals involved in it, the easier it will be to conduct a good session.

9

The Art of Questioning

The Purpose of Questioning

Questions represent one of the most important and widely used tools of an instructor. They may be used for the following purposes:

a) To arouse interest and curiosity. At the beginning of a session, questions can be used to gain interest and focus the attention of the group on the subject.

b) To stimulate discussion. Questions that are thought-provoking will get reactions.

c) To channel thinking. By skillful questioning, you can steer the group to the objective you have established. You can keep them on the right track and guide their thinking. Also, a series of well-prepared questions can help the group move from the known to the unknown.

d) To determine how well the group understands the material. By weighing the responses to a question, you can determine if the group has absorbed what you have been presenting. It also gives you an opportunity to correct any misconceptions or to elaborate on points that need further clarification.

e) To get the attention of a particular individual.

f) To help a timid person arrange and express his thoughts.

Types of Questions

There are three general types of questions that can be used. First, there's the overhead question. This is a question that is directed to the entire group. Anyone may answer. Its primary function is to stimulate group thinking and discussion. You may get an answer from one person at a time or several may attempt to answer.

Second, there is the direct question addressed to a specific individual.

The third type of question is the rhetorical. It is addressed to the entire group, but an answer is not expected, the answer being implicit in the question. ("We don't want to spend all night on this aspect of the problem, do we?" is an example.) It is used especially to stimulate thinking, often at the beginning of a session.

Characteristics of Effective Questions

No matter which type of question you use, it should require some thought in order to be answered. This usually rules out questions which may be answered by a simple "yes" or "no." You want to develop constructive thinking and eliminate guess-work: thus, each question should have a specific purpose and be pertinent to the subject.

Questions should be briefly put and easily understood. A long question is confusing: your listeners will either forget the first part, or become so involved in thinking about it that they won't hear the entire question. To be understood you should express the question in the language of the group. If you feel that they don't understand the question, rephrase it or approach it from a different angle.

Each question should be restricted to one main thought: don't link several questions together. Also, be certain the question is neither too general nor too broad.

Asking Questions

Although the art of questioning is being considered as a separate item here, in practice your questions should be a natural part of your presentation. You should plan the questions you want to ask, but you should be flexible and adjust to the responses given by the participants. You may have to change some questions; you may not use all that you have prepared.

Whether you use a direct or an overhead question, address the question to the entire group. If you want a certain person to respond, name him *after* you've framed the question. This insures that the entire group will think about the question and the answer. If you give one individual's name first, only that person may think about the answer.

Distribute the questions among the group; don't restrict them to one or two individuals. Don't establish a definite pattern— participants will soon figure this out, and won't do much thinking about the subject until their turn is due to come.

Questions which arouse antagonism should not be used. These will cause the group to draw away from you.

Avoid questions which you know the group cannot answer. Don't put an individual on the spot by directing a question to him that you know he can't answer.

Ask the questions in a friendly, sincere manner. Your tone and manner should be such that the participants are encouraged to express themselves. Your manner should encourage confidence and understanding, and tone of voice is very important. If your tone suggests indifference, lack of confidence, distrust, sarcasm, or a know-it-all attitude, your question will not be effective. A friendly tone and a pleasant expression can help insure the best reception to your question.

Examples of effective questions are:

How does this problem look to you?

This is an open question in that it invites the individual to express what he thinks. It doesn't make him feel that he must conform to a certain pattern, or answer in a certain way.

How did you work out your solution?

This gives direction, and encourages the student to think that his solution has merit.

What would you say the first step should be?

This appeals to reason.

What are your reasons?

Can you give us a specific example?

Suppose we did this—what would happen?

Are there any other factors to be considered?

Handling Responses

How you handle the responses to your questions is very important. You can alienate an individual or the entire group if you aren't careful. Incorrect handling of a response may cause an individual to withdraw mentally from the session.

First, of course, you must give the individual time to answer. Remember, he has to think about it and formulate his answer. If you think that the question is not understood, rephrase it, or break the question down into smaller parts. If you've used an overhead question, don't worry about the lack of immediate response: someone will eventually break the silence. It may seem like a long time to you, but actually it isn't. Don't answer the question yourself. If you start answering your own questions without giving the group time to think, you will encourage the class to rely on you for all of the answers.

You should acknowledge all responses. If the answer is good, praise the individual or otherwise comment favorably: "That's a good point"; "That's important"; "You're on the right track." If the answer is not clear to you or if it's incorrect, do some additional questioning. By skillful questioning, you can get the student to elaborate on his answer. You can also "lead" him to the discovery that his answer is not correct or that there's a flaw in his reasoning. You can rephrase your question or ask a leading question. Your main purpose is to help him with his thinking—not to embarrass him or make him feel foolish.

You can get comments from others by directing questions to individuals or to the group as a whole.

A relay question can be used to get comments from everyone. This is a question you ask of everyone, one at a time. It's an effective technique to get everyone involved, and to help the timid person break the ice.

Handling Questions

Some questions will be directed to you. Many of these you will answer immediately; others you won't answer at all. You can expect to get two types of questions: those that are legitimate requests for information, and those intended to embarrass you. It is sometimes difficult to distinguish between them. However, as you become familiar with the individuals in the group, you will learn how to handle both them and their questions.

In answering questions, you should be certain that you reply to the question that was asked. Don't evade the question and don't ramble. Be as specific as possible. If the question is not clear to you, ask to have the question repeated or ask for additional information—perhaps an example or illustration.

99

In a small group, everyone will probably hear the question. But if the question is not heard by everyone, it should be repeated.

Don't answer the question so quickly that you give the impression that the individual himself should have known the answer. On the other hand, don't take too long. Take just long enough to indicate that you are giving thought to your answer. Then state your answer in well-chosen words.

The reverse question technique can be used if you want to get the individual or the group to do some thinking. This means that you should direct the question back to the individual with an appropriate comment. For example, "That's a good question. I'd like to hear your comments on it, Mr. Smith"; or, "What would some of you suggest?" You can summarize the answers or opinions, and add to them after the members of the group have expressed their views.

You may be asked a question you can't, or don't want to, answer. If you can't answer because you don't know, simply state that you don't know. You can offer to find out and let them know (be certain that you do), or you can ask if anyone in the group knows. If you know there's someone in the group who knows, you can refer the question to him. A comment such as, "I don't know, but Mr. _____ has had considerable experience in that line. Let's ask him." Most individuals will respond. There's nothing wrong with admitting you don't know, or in calling on someone else to assist you in answering, but don't do it too frequently. If you do, the group's opinion of you and their respect for your knowledge diminish sharply.

If it's a question that will be answered later in the session or in another session, tell the group so. Just be certain that you do cover it. You must guard against ever giving the impression that you are trying to sweep a question "under the rug."

If it's an irrelevant question or one you shouldn't answer, simply state that it is something which does not pertain to the current subject, or it's something you are not qualified to answer. Do this as tactfully as you can.

Keeping your temper and not becoming upset or impatient are important to you as an instructor. Don't forget that what may seem to be an inappropriate or ill-timed question to you may in reality be an indication of a need you have overlooked. The manner in which you handle questions can have an important influence on your effectiveness as an instructor.

10

Evaluation

Why Evaluate?

When the session is over and the last participant has left, you will ask yourself, "How did I do?" As a conscientious instructor concerned with doing a good job, the answer is important to you. You want to know if your instruction was effective. You will ask yourself questions such as, "Did the participants understand what was presented?"; "Did they leave with a feeling of having learned something?"; "Would different techniques have been more effective?"; "Did everyone participate?"

All of this is what may be termed a "post-mortem," and it is necessary for maximum effectiveness of a program. It is an attempt to determine whether or not the session or sessions have met the established objectives. This evaluation can lead to a change of method or a change of content. It is something which is done during, as well as after, a session. Furthermore, it is done no matter how many times a particular subject is presented.

The evaluation will help you to analyze the effectiveness of your presentation and to determine how you should improve your knowledge and skills.

What Is Evaluated?

In making the evaluation you should consider:

(a) Content. Did the material covered in the session meet the needs of the group? Did you have to adjust the material to meet the group's needs?

(b) Methods. Were the methods used the best for the subject and the group? Did the methods stimulate the individuals? Did the group have opportunities to see, hear, discuss, do?

(c) Presentation. Was the material presented logically? Did you build on what was known? Were your objectives achieved?

(d) Time. Were you able to present the material adequately in the alloted time?

(e) Atmosphere. Was a friendly atmosphere established and maintained so that the participants were receptive to learning?

In the light of your answers to these questions, you can adjust your program to its advantage.

How to Evaluate

Both you and the individuals in your group can contribute to the evaluation. During the session, you can evaluate the reaction of the group as you are presenting material. You should be alert for signs of agreement, disagreement, bewilderment. Facial expressions will help you. You must also be able to discern a change in attitude, an improvement or development of a skill or ability, or an increase in knowledge among the participants. If you have established realistic objectives, you should be able to evaluate the session by asking yourself, "Are the objectives being achieved?" During your evaluation of a session or an entire program, you will want to answer questions such as:

Were the objectives achieved, and to what degree? (If not, why not?)

Were the students' expectations met? How do you know?

What were some of the indications of changes in knowledge, skills, or attitudes?

What training methods worked well? Why? Which ones were not successful? Why?

Were facilities and equipment satisfactory? How might they be improved?

What improvements can be made in the material?

Did everyone participate?

Did I stimulate discussion?

The individuals in the group will be making their evaluation, too. They will be evaluating you, your presentation, and the material. Some of their reactions will be revealed in the discussion periods, during breaks, or after sessions. Although you learn a great deal from the group in this way, you may not get a complete evaluation. You can learn more by distributing a questionnaire to be completed by each participant. The questionnaire may be distributed after each session, midway through a series of sessions, or at the end of the entire program, but having individuals answer questionnaires during the course of the program increases their interest and participation. It helps them feel that they are a part of the program and that you are interested in presenting what they want. Some questions that could be included in a questionnaire are:

On what subjects or in what areas do you need further information?

Are your expectations being met? If not, please explain.

What aspects of your job can you do better, thanks to the program?

In which aspects of your job do you still need help?

What comments do you have concerning the facilities and equipment used for this program?

In what specific areas could improvement be made?

Don't make the questionnaire too long or too difficult to complete. Also, don't overdo the use of questionnaires; too many may make the technique ineffective.

If you distribute a questionnaire at the end of the program, you can ask the individuals to take it with them and mail it back to you within two weeks. To insure this, the questionnaire can be designed as a self-mailer, or a self-addressed, stamped envelope can be distributed with each questionnaire. A sample questionnaire is shown in Figure 15.

The Value of Tests

One method of evaluation is the use of tests. However, tests must be prepared very carefully if they are to accomplish their purpose. Also, the manner in which tests are given and used can affect the reaction to them.

Consider first the purpose of a test. It is to measure performance by the individual; therefore, it can consist of any device that will accomplish this. Correctly designed and administered, a test can be an effective "tool" because it can:

a) determine how much the individual has learned;

b) challenge the individual;

c) aid in the learning process by pointing out errors and weaknesses;

d) summarize a unit of teaching.

Questionnaire

Student Evaluation:

Your frank and honest evaluation will help us improve all of our courses. Please answer all questions as specifically and completely as possible. Your suggestions will be appreciated very much. (Use the reverse side if necessary.) The evaluation need not be signed.

Title of course

Did the course meet your expectations? Please explain.

What else, if anything, would you like to have covered in a program of this type?

What specific improvements could be made?

Was there any conflicting instruction? In what sessions?

How has this program helped you?

Would you recommend this course to others? Why or why not?

What other comments or suggestions do you have?

Instructor's name
Date of completion of this form

Thank you for taking the time to complete this evaluation.

FIGURE 15. Questionnaire

How to Use Tests

Tests exist for the learner—not for the instructor. They should help the learner to measure his accomplishments and to assess his remaining needs. Adults like to know how they are doing, but they tend to shy away from tests and grades if these are to be used for comparative evaluation. They have a fear of not doing as well as the others. And such comparison is not important: what *is* important is that the individual find out for himself what he knows and what he needs to know . . . what he can do now, and what he wants to learn to do better in the future.

Adults will make their own self-evaluation based on a test. After a test has been given and corrected, adults should be encouraged to review the material covered in it. This review should be made *before* the papers are returned. (If test papers are returned first, the individuals check to see what question or questions they missed. They learn nothing from this, except that they missed Question 2, and they probably couldn't tell you now what Question 2 was about. Many will not care to review, particularly if they did well on the test.)

In conducting the review, the instructor should go over the content of the test—not necessarily following the test format. Use the review session as an opportunity to restate material in a different way. Don't call on individuals to answer questions in the order in which they were printed, or according to how the individuals are seated. This will not stimulate discussion, but will rather encourage each person to count ahead to see which question *he* will have to answer. Consequently, he will pay little attention to anything else.

If a large percentage of the group missed a certain question, it may indicate a poorly worded question or a need for additional information. You should concentrate on this area in your review.

Characteristics of an Effective Test

An effective test is one in which questions, statements, or problems are stated in a clear, definite manner. It is advisable to have someone other than the instructor review the test to insure that the language is clear. Remember: "Any question that can be misunderstood, will be misunderstood."

The test should be constructed so that it does not test an individual's memory, but rather measures his ability to apply his knowledge to practical situations. The test should be easy to score, and should permit uniformity in grading.

Validity and Reliability of Tests

In the construction of any type of measuring instrument, the trainer must always consider two factors: validity and reliability.

A test is a *valid* appraisal instrument when—and only when—it measures what it claims to measure. It is the dual responsibility of the test constructor, first, to analyze the particular ability or skill presented during the course of the training, and then to structure the test to measure the various aspects of that ability or skill, thus insuring a valid test.

The reliability of the test merits equal consideration. A test is said to be reliable if it consistently yields the same results when repeated measurements are taken of trainees under the same conditions. If a trainee receives a score of 120 on an intelligence test, for example, he should receive approximately the same score when an equivalent form of the test is given several weeks later.

Measuring validity and reliability involves the use of statistical methods. These methods are explained in depth in many educational statistic and test-and-measurement texts, to which the interested reader is referred.

Types of Tests

There are three types of test: oral, written, and performance. Oral tests are used in practically every training session. They consist of the direct questions you ask the participants to answer in the course of the program.

Written tests may be made up of essay (subjective) questions or objective questions.

The performance test, as the name indicates, involves actual doing by a participant (or by all participants). It is the most direct method of testing an individual's ability, and should be used whenever possible.

Some of the advantages of performance tests are:

1) Individuals like them—they enjoy "doing," applying what they have learned.

2) Bluffing is almost impossible.

3) Specific difficulties are readily revealed and corrective action can be taken immediately.

4) They are practically the only means of discovering whether an individual does *all* aspects of a job correctly.

5) They are practically the only way of revealing whether an individual becomes emotionally upset under pressure of actually doing the job, or in being observed.

Some disadvantages of performance tests include:

1) They may be difficult to set up properly.

2) They require considerably more time than any other type of test.

3) They may be difficult to administer because of tool and equipment requirements.

4) They are difficult to administer to large groups. The leader must observe the performance of each participant closely. (This difficulty may be alleviated in part by the use of assistants.)

Essay Tests

The general term "essay test" is used to describe free-response examinations. In the broad sense, an essay test is any examination in which the person being tested composes his own response, stated in his own way. Such tests are also referred to as subjective tests.

The advantages of essay tests are:

1) They are relatively easy to construct and administer.

2) They are effective in measuring an individual's ability to organize and express his thoughts.

Disadvantages are:

1) Individuals who cannot express themselves well in writing may be unfairly penalized, even though they know the subject matter well.

2) The tests usually require considerably more time to complete, since the person being tested must organize his answer and present it in detail.

3) These tests also require more time for evaluation and grading. Also, they provide an opportunity for an individual to bluff.

4) The answers are difficult to evaluate objectively. Sometimes the person bluffing does it so cleverly that he receives an undeserved good grade. Also, the best grades usually go to those who answered exactly as the instructor would—even though other answers, reached with proper reasoning, might be as good or even better.

In constructing essay-type tests, you should observe the following:

1) Questions should be worded so that their meaning is clear.

2) Questions should be direct and specific.

3) Words such as "why," "explain clearly," "outline," "define," "compare" should be used in the questions to indicate the *form* of response expected.

4) Questions that involve several points should be subdivided.

5) Questions should be designed to test the individual's *understanding* of the text material, rather than his memory.

6) Avoid questions that ask, "In your opinion, what is ....," "What are your thoughts about.........," "Give your ideas about.........," since any answer to such a question is necessarily correct.

Objective Tests

The objective test was conceived and developed in an effort to overcome the disadvantages encountered in the use of the subjective (essay) test.

The term "objective" refers to the method of scoring, rather than to the nature of the test. In evaluating an objective test, the rules are so defined that two trainers should be able to score the same test and get identical results.

Although relatively new, the objective test has already gained wide acceptance among educators and trainers. This does not mean that objective tests are superior to subjective tests for all situations. Subjective examinations will continue to enjoy wide use, often side by side with objective examinations. The point is that objective tests do have some advantages which make them especially efficient in certain circumstances.

Four types of objective tests will be explained: the true-and-false test; the multiple-choice test; the matching test; and the completion (or recall) test.

True-and-False Tests

For many instructors, the true-false item has always been the main instrument of objective measurement. However, of all the techniques of objective evaluation, the true-false test is the least flexible, the most limited in what it can measure, and one of the most difficult to handle effectively.

In such tests, statements are given which may be either true or false. The trainee indicates his response with a plus or a minus, a "T" or an "F," or in words (true or false; yes or no).

The advantages of a true-false test are:

1) The test can be corrected quickly.

2) The answer can be evaluated objectively; it is either true or false.

Disadvantages of a true-false test are:

1) Construction of a true-false test is difficult. It requires considerable skill to write items that are either entirely true or false, without being too obvious. Phrasing of questions is critical: one misplaced word, or even punctuation mark, can cause confusion.

2) The test encourages guessing, and, therefore, may not be reliable for measuring an individual's achievement.

3) Because it is easy to prepare a "trick" question—and, unfortunately, this is often done—many people mistrust such tests.

In constructing a true-false test, you should:

1) Be certain each statement contains only one point.

2) Avoid catch or trick questions.

3) Avoid use of words such as *always, never, usually,* or *sometimes.* They tend to give away the response to the statement in some cases and, in others, give the impression that it is a "trick" question.

4) Be certain the statement covers an important point, not an unimportant detail.

5) Arrange true and false statements in random order.

6) Use common words and simple sentences.

7) Use only statements that are definitely true or false.

8) Use a large number of statements.

9) Arrange the statements in the order of difficulty.

Multiple-Choice Tests

The preferred form of an objective test is the multiple-choice examination. The reason for this is that multiple-choice items can measure most of the important educational results, including knowledge, understanding, and judgment.

Almost any ability or understanding which can be measured by another form of examination item—objective or subjective; completion, short answer, true-false, or essay—can be measured by multiple-choice items.

A multiple-choice item is less vulnerable to chance errors due to guessing than are other forms of objective tests, such as matching or true-false. It requires that the individual select the best answer from a list of four or five possible answers, the problem being stated in the form of an incomplete statement or question.

The advantages of the multiple-choice test are:

1) The test measures what the trainee recognizes, rather than what he recalls.

2) It can be used to test the individual's ability to interpret facts, and to apply what he knows.

3) The possibility of guessing is minimal.

114

4) The test may be corrected quickly.

5) Evaluating the test is completely objective.

The disadvantages of the multiple-choice test are:

1) The test takes considerable time to prepare.

2) It is difficult to write test items so that the wrong answers are plausible though incorrect.

3) Care must be taken to avoid including more than one correct answer.

Before explaining the guidelines for writing the multiple-choice items that make up this type of objective test, several important terms applicable to multiple-choice item construction will be defined. These items are: stem, option, key, distracter, and item.

1) A multiple-choice *stem* is the introductory question or incomplete statement for which the trainee chooses a response or a completion from two or more options.

2) An *option* is a response to the stem in a multiple-choice item. Each stem requires two or more options, or responses; four is a common, workable number.

3) The *key* is the one correct reponse (or option) to a multiple-choice stem.

4) A *distracter* is any incorrect response (or option) to a stem.

5) An *item* consists of the stem and all its options or responses.

Here are two examples of a multiple-choice item. One has a stem which is an incomplete statement; the other, a stem which is a question. A check-mark indicates the key, or correct response.

An example with the stem in the form of an incomplete statement:

The name of the author of *Hamlet* is—

A. Ben Jonson

B. William Blake

C. Matthew Arnold

D. William Shakespeare √

The same example, but with the stem in the form of a question:

Which one of the following was the author of *Hamlet*?

A. Ben Jonson

B. William Blake

C. Matthew Arnold

D. William Shakespeare √

In preparing multiple-choice items, you should:

1) Avoid using grammatical constructions that may give a clue to the correct answer.

2) Use simple, unambiguous words. Avoid verbal tricks and words that are too colorful.

3) Be precise in wording an item.

4) A particular item should not interlock with a previous item or a later item, thus providing a clue to the correct response.

5) Avoid an incomplete or a too general stem that necessitates unrelated options.

6) Avoid any item which can be answered solely by general intelligence, without any knowledge of the material being tested.

7) Try to avoid the word "not" in the stem.

8) Avoid unnecessary words or sentences in the stem.

9) Make all of the options, or choices, parallel both in grammar and in point of view.

10) Avoid overuse of the phrase "none of these" as an option.

11) For consistency, supply the same number of options in each item of an examination.

12) Refrain from the use of inappropriate or ridiculous distracters.

13) Avoid options which contain the word "always" or "never" or similar words.

14) Try to keep all options about the same length.

15) Be wary of using two opposites as options, when one of the opposites is the key.

16) When the key is an absolutely correct answer, make the distracters (incorrect options) completely wrong, but still plausible.

Matching Tests

The matching test is a special form of the multiple-choice item. In a matching test, an individual is given two columns of items and is required to match or pair each item in one column with an associated item in the other. For example, he may be asked to match:

1) Short questions with answers.

2) Causes with effects.

3) Parts of mechanical units with their proper names.

4) Names of tools with their uses.

5) Problems with their solutions.

6) Signs or symbols with their meanings.

The advantages of a matching test are:

1) The test provides a check of the individual's knowledge of nomenclature.

2) The test requires the individual to think.

3) The individual's knowledge of the function of parts can be checked.

4) It is possible to check relationships.

The disadvantages of a matching test are:

1) It is difficult to avoid the misinterpretation of certain items.

2) It requires much "hunt and find."

In constructing matching questions, a good procedure is to:

1) Write down a series of statements concerning the items to be covered.

2) Separate the subject and predicate of each sentence.

3) Arrange the subject and predicate parts of these sentences in two columns. Place a checking space before each of the subjects. Place a number before each predicate. Mix up the order of the items so that most of the predicates are not opposite their respective subjects.

Here are some standards against which you may check your matching questions:

1) Do not use too many items: ten to fifteen items make a good test.

2) Be certain only one correct combination can be made between items in the first list and those in the second. Check every possible combination of items to be certain that an item on one list can be used properly with only one item in the other list.

3) Include from one to three more items in the numbered list than in the other to eliminate guessing.

4) Alphabetize the items in one of the lists; number the items in the other.

5) Mix up the items so they are not in sequence as numbered, and so most items are not opposite the corresponding ones.

6) Keep all items of the test on the same page.

7) Use only related materials in any one exercise.

Completion or Recall Tests

The completion test consists of free-response items. This type of objective test is generally used to measure educational outcomes that are psychologically simpler than those that are measured by the subjective (essay) type of examination. In the completion test, an individual is required to insert a word, a phrase, or a figure which is missing from a statement.

The advantages of a completion test are:

1) The participant does not need to do a great deal of writing.

2) The test checks the trainee's knowledge of nomenclature.

The disadvantages of a completion test are:

1) The test emphasizes memory.

2) Speed in reading can be a factor in effective completion of the test.

3) It is difficult to word sentences so that only one response is correct.

Standards for the preparation of completion tests are:

1) Omit only key words, not long phrases. The omission should be three words or less.

2) Construct the items so that there is only one correct response.

3) Do not use sentences taken directly from the text material or summary notes.

4) Place the blank spaces near or at the end of the sentence.

5) Make all blank spaces the same length. This practice avoids giving a clue to the length of the word or words in the correct answer.

6) Be certain to provide adequate space for responses.

In conclusion, evaluation by you, by the group, and by the use of tests should be integrated into all that you do. It should be an important aspect of any program so that you can learn while you instruct, thus improving yourself while helping others to improve.

Figure 16 is a form that you may find helpful in evaluating your performance.

Evaluation Form

After each session, review this self-evaluation form. Be honest with yourself. This self-evaluation will help you improve your presentation.

Material

Was my material appropriate for the group?
Was it well-organized?
Did I make my objectives known?
Did I explain and emphasize main points?
Did I achieve my objectives?
Were my communication aids effective?
Were my handouts adequate?
Did I summarize?
Were the case studies or problems of value?

Presentation

Did I secure the attention and interest of the group?
Did I give a coherent presentation?
Did I motivate the group?
Did I use the communication aids effectively?
Did I establish rapport with the group?
Did I encourage participation?
Did I use simple, understandable, correct language?
Did I use the proper tone of voice?
Were my gestures meaningful?
Did I "ah," "er," or use words such as "well," "now," excessively?
Could I be heard and understood?
Did I use proper questioning techniques?
Was my demonstration correct and well-organized?
Did I make the best use of the time available?

Facilities

Were the physical arrangements satisfactory?
Did I keep adequate records?

FIGURE 16. Evaluation Form

A Word to the Instructor

This book has sought to give you information on good instruction techniques and practices. As you use these techniques, you will become proficient in them. You can also learn from observing others, picking up good points from them. However, do not follow them blindly. What may work for one person may not work for you. If you have the opportunity to observe a successful instructor, try to analyze *why* he was good. Use this information to improve what you do—but be yourself.

Remember, instructors teach people, not subjects. Your use of your knowledge will be classified as skillful when you are able to communicate that knowledge effectively—that is, to meet your students' needs.

You are on your way to being a capable, conscientious instructor. Good luck and smooth sailing!